PRAISE FOR

THE FIRE OF HIS HOLINESS

It is a marvelous thing when the living God interrupts your plans! This book can help you to embrace the fullness and satisfaction you desire out of life by encouraging you to yield to God's holy love.

Ché Ahn

SENIOR PASTOR, HARVEST ROCK CHURCH
PRESIDENT, HARVEST INTERNATIONAL MINISTRIES (HIM)
PASADENA, CALIFORNIA

A profound message written with simplicity and depth that will have life-changing effects on all who read it.

Beth Alves

PRESIDENT, INTERCESSORS INTERNATIONAL, INC., BULVERDE, TEXAS

Sergio Scataglini is that rare and treasured individual: an excellent scholar and theologian who ministers powerfully in the Holy Spirit. His powerful testimony and helpful insights are presented with a pleasant and joyful personality.

John Arnott

SENIOR PASTOR, TORONTO AIRPORT CHRISTIAN FELLOWSHIP
TORONTO, ONTARIO, CANADA

I have known Sergio Scataglini as his pastor and friend. I know him, love him and trust him. I pray that his sincere account of what God has done in his life and ministry will touch all who read these pages. I pray that all of us will be filled with the authentic holiness of God.

Paul Cedar
CHAIRMAN, MISSION AMERICA, PALM DESERT, CALIFORNIA

The Fire of His Holiness is a timely, doctrinally sound message with the penetrating power of experience.

Frank Damazio
PASTOR, CITY BIBLE CHURCH, PORTLAND, OREGON

Sergio Scataglini, who lives in the midst of the fiery Argentine revival, will set readers ablaze with this book. Prepare yourself to enter *The Fire of His Holiness*.

Stephen L. Hill
EVANGELIST, FOLEY, ALABAMA

This book is living flame! You will never be the same after opening the pages of *The Fire of His Holiness*.

Cindy Jacobs
COFOUNDER, GENERALS OF INTERCESSION
COLORADO SPRINGS, COLORADO

Sergio Scataglini demonstrates clearly that "mostly holy" isn't going to cut it any longer in these troubled times. To paraphrase our Lord, "Satan would fry you up like trout if I let him." Now is the time to get out of the frying pan of this world and jump into the fire of the holiness of God.

Dutch Sheets
AUTHOR, *INTERCESSORY PRAYER*
SENIOR PASTOR, SPRINGS HARVEST FELLOWSHIP
COLORADO SPRINGS, COLORADO

I laughed, then I cried as the transparency of a surrendered servant of God poured out of the pages of this book. I absolutely loved the message and the messenger. Don't miss out on the profound spiritual truths of *The Fire of His Holiness*.

Alice Smith
INTERNATIONAL PRAYER COORDINATOR, U. S. PRAYER TRACK
A. D. 2000 & BEYOND MOVEMENT
HOUSTON, TEXAS

It is as if the finger of God tattooed the walls of Sergio Scataglini's heart. Then Sergio ripped the pages from that fleshly tablet and laid them before us, pasted raw into this book. God said to Sergio, "Holiness," so Sergio says to us, "Holiness." Others have said the same thing, but not with the gripping conviction found here. No one can talk as convincingly of the fire as one who has been "burned." The fire of God has touched Sergio; he has joined Isaiah in the brotherhood of the burning. Isaiah said he saw the Lord high and lifted up, and an angel took a hot coal from the altar and touched it to his lips. Sergio, your lips are on fire! And so is this book. May we all be ignited!

Tommy Tenney
THE GOD CHASERS NETWORK
PINEVILLE, LOUISIANA

Sergio Scataglini has written a book to explain more carefully the supernatural nature of the conversion experience that all must have to be truly born again. Many Americans have simply joined the Church, but this author tells us that we must meet God in a true way through His Son Jesus Christ, and those who are not truly born again do not belong to Him. For all those who want to know more of God, *The Fire of His Holiness* will tell you how to die to self and walk again in the newness of life.

Elmer L. Towns
DEAN, SCHOOL OF RELIGION, LIBERTY UNIVERSITY
LYNCHBURG, VIRGINIA

This book is the testimony of a man who burns with the fire of holiness. Pastor Sergio Scataglini is a dear friend and a great man of God. We have known each other since our days as students in Bible College and to this day I enjoy his friendship. His life is a blessing to me and to all of the Body of Christ. In this book, Sergio presents a deep message which is central to the Christian faith. This message will move you and bring you first to the altar of consecration and brokenness, then lift you to a new level of spiritual sensitivity and victory in every area of your life. Prepare now to die to yourself that you may truly live!

Claudio Freidzon

PASTOR, KING OF KINGS CHURCH
BUENOS AIRES, ARGENTINA

THE FIRE OF HIS
HOLINESS

PREPARE
YOURSELF TO
ENTER GOD'S
PRESENCE

SERGIO SCATAGLINI

Renew

A Division of Gospel Light
Ventura, California, U.S.A.

Published by Renew Books
A Division of Gospel Light
Ventura, California, U.S.A.
Printed in U.S.A.

Renew Books is a ministry of Gospel Light, an evangelical Christian publisher dedicated to serving the local church. We believe God's vision for Gospel Light is to provide church leaders with biblical, user-friendly materials that will help them evangelize, disciple and minister to children, youth and families.

It is our prayer that this Renew book will help you discover biblical truth for your own life and help you meet the needs of others. May God richly bless you.

For a free catalog of resources from Renew Books and Gospel Light please call your Christian supplier, or contact us at 1-800-4-GOSPEL.

Cover Design by Kevin Keller
Interior Design by Robert Williams
Edited by Kyle Duncan

Library of Congress Cataloging-in-Publication Data
Scataglini, Sergio, 1957–
    The fire of His holiness / Sergio Scataglini.
        p.   cm.
    ISBN 0-8307-2378-1 (trade)
    1. Christian life—Assemblies of God authors. 2. Holiness—Christianity.
    3. Scataglini, Sergio, 1957–   . I. Title.
    BV4510.2.S2813   1999
    289.9'4'092   99-31475
    [B]—DC21   CIP

3 4 5 6 7 8 9 10 11 12 13 14 15 / 05 04 03 02 01 00

Rights for publishing this book in other languages are contracted by Gospel Literature International (GLINT). GLINT also provides technical help for the adaptation, translation and publishing of Bible study resources and books in scores of languages worldwide. For further information, write to GLINT at P.O. Box 4060, Ontario, CA 91761-1003, U.S.A. You may also send E-mail to Glintint@aol.com, or visit their web site at www.glint.org.

THIS BOOK IS DEDICATED
TO MY WIFE KATHY:
FRIEND, PARTNER IN MINISTRY
AND COMPANION IN
DOING GOD'S WILL.

CONTENTS

Foreword by C. Peter Wagner 13

Acknowledgments 17

Introduction 19

*If you are not seeking the fire of His
holiness, you are in a different movement than the one Jesus began.*

Chapter 1 23
Apprehended by His Fire

*The Lord had different plans for me.
He did not regard my agenda—He
ripped it to pieces!*

Chapter 2 33
The Fear of the Lord

*The Lord spoke to me and said clear-
ly, "98% holiness is not enough."*

Chapter 3 41
Living Close to the Flames: Revival in Argentina

*It is wonderful to pray and believe
for revival, but it is equally important to be willing to pay the price for
revival when it happens.*

Chapter 4 51
Anointed for Holiness

*The Lord tests those who seek the fire
of His holiness.*

Chapter 5 57

A Fresh Manifestation of the Fire of God

> *The Holy Spirit wants to get our*
> *attention, grab us with His love and*
> *tear out the sin in our lives.*

Chapter 6 67

Our Evangelical Sins

> *The Christian life begins with death,*
> *and then it moves on to resurrection*
> *in Christ.*

Chapter 7 79

Self-Examination and the Call to Repentance

> *Purity is by faith. It is not self-*
> *discipline, but a miracle from heaven.*

Chapter 8 89

False Conversions and God's Fire

> *We must lead people to Christ by*
> *teaching them that they need a*
> *Savior, not just a blessing.*

Chapter 9 105

Warning Signs of Spiritual Decadence

> *God gives us signs of danger to alert*
> *us to things that will wear us out,*
> *such as decadence or apathy.*

Chapter 10 119

A Change of Clothes for the High Priest

> *The Lord wants to change our filthy*
> *garments and cause us to live with a*
> *completely clean conscience.*

Chapter 11 129
The Dynamics of Temptation

> *Satan cannot do anything to us if we*
> *do not give him room! The problem*
> *is that by being human, we give him*
> *a place to work.*

Chapter 12 139
Preparing the Altar for the Fire

> *We must prepare the altar of our*
> *lives if we want to be ready for the*
> *fire of God to fall upon us.*

Chapter 13 155
Keep the Fire Burning

> *How do we maintain a fire for holi-*
> *ness? The One who calls us is faith-*
> *ful, and He will do it through us.*

Chapter 14 171
How Desperate Are You for the Fire?

> *You need a certain audacity of faith*
> *to receive a miracle from God.*

Appendix 183

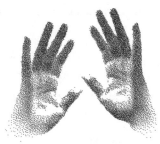

FOREWORD

I suspect you have been hearing more about holiness in the last couple of years than you have ever heard before.

By this I do not mean that Christians have ever dropped the biblical word "holiness" from their vocabulary. However, the tendency has been to emphasize the holiness of God or, when applying holiness to ourselves, to pass it off rather lightly as something that would be nice to have a bit more of but not to worry much about.

Things are changing—rapidly. The Holy Spirit has started speaking to the churches about holiness with an intensity not previously seen, at least in our generation. The subject is being highlighted in messages, in conferences, in articles, in books, in classrooms across regional and denominational lines. There is no question that God intends to raise the whole Body of Christ to new levels of purity, righteousness and obedience to His complete will.

Sergio Scataglini has emerged as one of God's foremost leaders in this expanding season of holiness. I could not be more delighted and at the same time amazed. Sergio is my student—and more. He and his wife, Kathy, were members of the Sunday School class that I taught for many years. I feel like a father who didn't really know how his son would turn out. Then suddenly Sergio became an internationally recognized leader. Why? Because he allowed God to visit him with an awesome experience of personal holiness. He received God's supernatural anointing to communicate the message of holiness to the rest of the Body of Christ.

Why didn't God choose someone like Sergio Scataglini to present this message to us years ago? I'm not surprised that God would select someone who had been touched by the Argentine revival. In fact the major event of the early days of the Argentine revival took place in the church that Sergio now pastors in La Plata. At that time, his father and my friend, Alberto Scataglini, pastored the church in which Carlos Annacondia began to become a household name—first in Argentina, then throughout the world. But the Argentine revival was in its fifteenth year when God brought the message of holiness to the forefront through Sergio.

By way of answering my own question, my hypothesis would be that God wanted to be sure that a significant segment of the Body of Christ had corporately received the power of the Holy Spirit, that they were healing the sick and casting out demons, that large numbers of unsaved people were becoming disciples of Jesus Christ, that God's people understood the nature of the spiritual battle for extending the Kingdom and that they were on the right track. To this end, He selected and worked through such incredible leaders as Omar Cabrera, Carlos Annacondia, Eduardo Lorenzo, Claudio Freidzon, Edgardo Silvoso, Pablo Deiros, Pablo Bottari and others. Each one of them had a significant role to play in fanning the flames of revival in Argentina.

Now they all have powerful international ministries, but none of them has become known particularly for communicating the call of God to radical personal holiness.

Perhaps if holiness had become a primary theme of the revival in earlier days, it could have been seen as an end in itself. History has already recorded many instances of enthusiasm for holiness in the lives of believers ultimately becoming ingrown and self-serving and abandoning evangelization of the lost. This is the last thing that Argentina or the rest of the world needs. However, in the Argentine revival, the passion for seeing souls saved has become so firmly entrenched that a strong message of holiness would only continue to fan the flames. That is why Sergio Scataglini has called his book *The Fire of His Holiness.*

God has been raising up His army worldwide for the most explosive advance in all of history against the strongholds of the prince of the power of the air. This is why the Body of Christ needs to move to a new level, and that level is a total sell-out to personal holiness. I agree with Sergio that God's standard is not 98%, but nothing less than 100%.

The book you hold in your hands is a divinely empowered instrument to help take you to that level. You may not be thrust there through a single dramatic life-changing experience like the one that "floored" Sergio, but if you allow God the freedom to work in your life the way He desires, you definitely can attain that mark because it is God's will that you do.

My prayer is that, as you read this book, you will receive the full impartation of the fire of His holiness.

C. Peter Wagner

WAGNER LEADERSHIP INSTITUTE

ACKNOWLEDGMENTS

I want to acknowledge a group of godly people who have encouraged me and influenced my life in the pursuit of God, His commands and His Great Commission.

First, I must mention my parents, the Rev. Alberto J. Scataglini and Isabel, who instilled in me a deep respect for the things of God. Ed Silvoso took time to write to me, even as a teenager, and talk about the things of the Lord. He showed up while I was in college and in seminary and when I was newly married. He always had a good word and a challenge for me to keep God's priorities my priorities. Ed has been the most influential Christian leader in my life.

Wick Nease, a great man of God, invited me to travel with his family to the United States and then took time to follow up to see that my heart continued to stay tuned to God's. He has been a model of Christian character and stability for me. Dr. C. Peter Wagner is more than just a professor at Fuller Seminary to me and my wife. He and Doris were there for us when we were sent out into the world to minister. We value not only Peter's spiritual insights, but also his love and friendship.

One cannot be in touch with Carlos Annacondia and not be challenged! What an example of a godly man who has a heart for the lost. His simplicity and realness have been an inspiration for my life. And last, but certainly not least, I must mention my friend Claudio Freidzon. We have gone from being casual friends and roommates in Bible school to being fellow ministers and close friends with a common passion to see lives transformed by the anointing and fire of God. Claudio and his wife, Betty, have been a consistent influence in my life, encouraging me to live under God's anointing.

I want to say a special thank you to my children, Nathaniel, Jeremy and Miqueas, who are part of our ministry team. They are involuntary soldiers who have been drafted into this army to serve, and they are good troopers! They have been gracious in giving me (and Kathy) time and space to get this book written.

I also must mention my congregation and staff at Puerta del Cielo. The natural tendency is to *not* want the pastor to be gone. They have truly gone the second mile by providing spiritual covering through their signed commitments to pray and fast during each trip I made this past year. I must also say a big thank you to those ladies from the church (especially Marta, Lidia and Raquel) who prepared, cooked and brought us food so that we could get the book done! Your servant attitude and actions have blessed us!

Finally, I want to recognize my wife and partner in ministry, Kathy. She typed, transcribed, translated and patiently interpreted my material for this book, at times under heavy pressure. Without her, this book would not be in your hands.

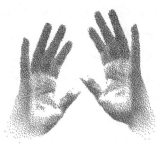

INTRODUCTION

Before you begin reading this book, let me warn you: *You will be challenged to change!* My dear brother and dear sister, if you feel satisfied with your walk with God, this book is *not* for you. This book is a combination of two things: a testimony of the direct intervention of God Almighty in my life and an instrument to impart the same to you!

This book is about holiness. You may ask, "Why should I read this book and add condemnation to my life? I do my best and fall upon the grace of God each Sunday to give me a clean slate for the week."

Let me ask you: Is that really as good as it gets?

It is true that this message is radical. Even more "way out there," however, is the fact that the majority of Christians preach and teach about abundant life in Jesus and miss the *first step* in the formula—death to their old life. *If you choose to go ahead and read this book, get ready to die!*

If you are dissatisfied with your Christian walk and desire to experience true victory, this book is for you. This book is not about a party but, rather, a funeral. But after death comes resurrection. It is about learning to die to oneself in order to be resurrected into an entirely new dimension of victorious Christian living.

I was a Christian for many years before I understood this process. It took this kernel of wheat a few years on the ground before I broke and died. I rode the normal Christian roller coaster of victory and defeat until May 1997. It was then that God apprehended me, baptized me with His fire and changed my life forever.

I had a defining encounter with Jesus.

If you think this happened to me because I am special, you are wrong. It did come, however, after many years of diligent seeking. I can relate to the Canaanite woman who approached Jesus with a request that He heal her daughter, only to receive discouraging answers again and again. Yet she never gave up (see Matt. 15:22-28).

You may say, "I come from the wrong city." So did Jesus. You may feel that you are a failure. Good! You are ready for the fire. You may be too proud to receive this fire—there is no remedy for you until you become broken.

We have found that many people are anxious to "get into the ministry" and find their function within the Body of Christ. Many Gideons get all excited about leading out the troops to defeat the enemy. There is nothing wrong with that, except it is important to look at the first part of the story as well as the ending.

Gideon's first action against the Midianites was to throw down the idols of Baal. The enemy called Gideon "Jerub-Baal," saying, "Let Baal contend with him." They named him this because he had kicked down all the idols of Baal overnight (see Judg. 6:32).

It is important to kick down our own idols before undertaking other spiritual battles. We must purify ourselves and our own realm before we try to win the world or accomplish great things for Christ.

If you are not seeking the fire of His holiness, you are in a different movement than the one Jesus began. "But what is the fire of God?" you may be asking. It is a transforming touch from God which causes you to hate sin with renewed vigor and, in faith, pursue holiness with intense passion. The result is a consuming love for God combined with a desire to see the lost come to Christ.

True Christianity is a religion of seekers. Most religious people will not feel comfortable with this book. They have learned to live the acceptable Christian life. The concepts in this book will definitely be troublesome for those who, in their religious zeal, "strain out a gnat but swallow a camel" (i.e., legalistic Christians). I recently heard this saying: The "good" is the greatest enemy of the "best."

My friend and renowned Argentine evangelist Ed Silvoso once told me, "God is comfortable when we are uncomfortable." I pray this book is one in which you and I will feel uncomfortable and God will feel right at home!

Sergio Scataglini
La Plata, Argentina

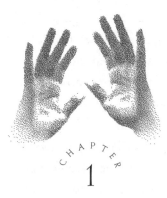

1

APPREHENDED BY HIS FIRE

I n early May 1997, I greeted my congregation in the city of La Plata, Argentina, and said, "I will come back to you in a week. I am going to see a couple of places of revival in the United States and I will bring back reports to you of what the Lord is doing in the world." Basically, as the senior pastor of a growing church in a suburb of Buenos Aires, I thought I was doing very well with the Lord. I thought all I needed was another touch from Him at these places of revival to strengthen my ministry.

However, there had been a cry, a very strange prayer I had been praying during the previous months. Several times while kneeling down I found myself praying, "Lord, if you are not going to bring another revival, take me home; I do not want to live anymore." And then I would rebuke my soul, because I have three little boys and a wonderful wife. Also, the ministry was not doing so bad. I thought, *I should not pray this way, because the Lord might answer my prayer by taking me home!*

Then the next day I would again find myself praying the same things. Then I realized that the Holy Spirit was putting a burden in my heart to see revival; I was developing a holy hunger for more of God. Scottish revivalist John Knox used to say, "Lord, give me Scotland or I will die."

Like many others, I was praying for revival, but I was not preparing for it. So I left for Pensacola, Florida, with the intention of visiting the revival at the Brownsville Assembly of God Church. This outpouring began on Father's Day, 1995. Since that time, three million people have visited the revival, while hundreds of thousands have recommitted or given their lives to Christ. This revival is marked by a deep call to repentance and holiness.

I was not disappointed by what I saw in Pensacola, and I rejoiced in the Lord as I witnessed hours of glory and blessing and hundreds of people who came to the front to receive Christ. I had a wonderful experience in Pensacola and felt that God had touched me. But I had no idea just how deeply. After visiting Pensacola for one night, I left very early the next morning for Elkhart, Indiana, where my wife's family lives and where our United States ministry office is located.

IN A RUSH TO GET TO THE NEXT MEETING

I arrived in Elkhart on a Friday, feeling refreshed and renewed. On Sunday morning, May 18, 1997, I went to bring a short greeting to the congregation at Zion Chapel, which had been our most recent home church when we lived in the States. I only had a few moments in the program, as they had another guest speaker that Sunday morning. It was not my turn to preach. As a matter of fact, I was supposed to leave very quickly and proceed to another church to preach. What I did not know is that the Lord had other plans.

I shared a greeting and then the pastor, Steve Chupp, said, "Let's ask Pastor Sergio to come up front so we can pray for him before he leaves to preach at Maranatha Fellowship, so he can carry fire to them." Those were his words. He called upon some young people to pray for me. How many of you know that young people are dangerous when they are in the hands of almighty God?

Several young people began to pray very calmly for me as I stood at the front of the sanctuary, just below the platform. Everything was quiet and nice and according to the church bulletin. As the young people began to pray for me, I closed my eyes; my mind was not on revival or anything else. I was in a rush to go to the next church to preach. Suddenly, my clasped hands began to shake, without my permission, and I could not control them.

I was raised in the Assemblies of God denomination; my father, Alberto Scataglini, was a prominent leader in the Assemblies of God in Argentina, serving as superintendent for the denomination and in several other capacities. In our denomination (and especially with the training I received from my father) when a pastor is on the platform, he is in control. We let the Lord use us, but we do not let things get out of hand. My father would say, "If the pastor loses control, what will happen to the rest of the congregation?"

That is wise advice. But in this case, for the first time ever, something was happening to me on the platform that I could not control. I thought, *This is out of place.* I opened my eyes and looked at the congregation before me. No one else's hands were shaking. I gripped my hands tightly, trying to stop the shaking— then my entire body began to shake. I remember locking my knees and making them really stiff in a vain attempt to stop my body from trembling. And then I fell on the floor.

Something strange was happening and I said to myself, *This is not right; I must get up.* I was lying on the floor, shaking uncontrollably. I was looking at the people and they were looking at me. No one was praying anymore! The pastor began to lead in a few songs. I guess they did not know what to do with me. One moment I was weeping and the next moment I was laughing. I felt very embarrassed, quite shocked and extremely happy, all at the same time.

I thought, *I must get out of here.* Three times I tried to get up. The third time two church leaders helped me to my feet. The associate pastor was next to me, holding me upright. The senior pastor stepped down from the platform and stood next to me.

Crying, I said, "Pastor, do not let me interrupt this meeting; please take me out of here." And this brother put his arm around my shoulder and said, "You are not interrupting, brother. This is the presence of God." His simple words were like a healing balm over my soul.

Finally, two men carried me out. I thought they were carrying me to a separate room. I desperately wanted to be alone with God. But they had the bad idea of sitting me in the front row. I continued shaking and every few minutes I would fall onto the floor and someone would come and pick me up and sit me back in the chair. Then I began to yell. I had my handkerchief and I put it over my mouth. And I said to myself, *I must not interrupt this meeting.* I restrained myself as much as I could, but the more I tried to control it, the stronger the waves of the Holy Spirit would come over me.

Later I learned that what I was experiencing was the fire of God. As I described in the introduction, this holy fire is a direct touch from God that motivates us to hate sin and love purity, with the purpose of winning souls for the Kingdom. It is a great passion to love God with all your heart, soul, mind and strength. I literally felt surges of power over my bones and my body. His glory was there. At the time, I did not know what to call it. However, I now realize that the fire of God is very biblical. In preparing the way for Christ, John the Baptist speaks about the baptism of fire when he says:

> I baptize you with water for repentance. But after me will come one who is more powerful than I, whose sandals I am not fit to carry. He will baptize you with the Holy Spirit and with fire (Matt. 3:11).

In the next verse, John says,

> His winnowing fork is in his hand, and he will clear his threshing floor, gathering his wheat into the barn and burning up the chaff with unquenchable fire (Matt. 3:12).

His fire is a holy fire; it is unquenchable and burns away the sin in our lives. And for those who do not submit to His fire, they will be utterly burned up, like the chaff. His fire will either burn in purification or in judgment.

FACING MY IN-LAWS

Without consulting me, someone went back to the church office and called the pastor of the other church that was expecting me to preach. The pastor was told, "It does not look like this fellow is going to make it today." It took me two weeks to get to that church to preach!

As I sat slumped in my seat in the first row, I was thinking, *Oh, what a wonderful wave of the power of God. I am sure that I will preach tremendously this morning.* Little did I know that it was an hour and a half past the time to preach. Toward the end of the service the pastor came and helped me up and put the microphone in front of me. He wanted me to minister to the congregation a little bit. As I tried to talk, I realized that I was not speaking correctly. I do know that I have a Spanish accent, but this was worse!

A few people came forward to be prayed for and I noticed that after I prayed for them, some were shaking like me. I was scared. It was too much for me for one day. Eventually a brother came and asked me a question that was a little embarrassing. He said, "Brother, do you need a ride home?"

And I said, "Yes, I think I do." I was driving a car that had been loaned to me, and this brother drove me home in it.

I had only one prayer as we were driving to my in-laws' house. As I continued to shake, cry and laugh, I pleaded, *Lord, please do not let my in-laws see me like this.* I was praying that they would not be there when I arrived. I really prayed this fervently. You see, my in-laws are godly people; I believe we are in the same Kingdom, just different neighborhoods. Over the years there had been some theological tension between us. I prayed, *Lord, do not let this cause any division.*

When we opened the door to my in-laws' house, standing right there before me were my mother-in-law and father-in-law. I could not walk very well, so the brother who had driven me home was sort of carrying me. I could not speak clearly but I remember saying to my mother-in-law, "Mom, I am okay; don't worry. But please do not look at me." And immediately my mother-in-law raised her hands to heaven and began to weep and praise God. She entered into a three-day fast for the glory of God. As I made my way to my room, to my great surprise I heard her say, "This is what we need in our churches!"

The brother began talking to them and explaining what had happened, which gave me an opportunity to sneak away to my room. I could not walk, but I could crawl. Slowly, I began my ascent up the stairs. I finally reached my room on the second floor and closed the door. I was so happy to be alone. I continued to shake and weep and I did not know what was happening. Two hours later, the signs ceased completely. There was no more shaking; everything was fine. I thought, *Boy, do I have things to tell my church in La Plata*, and I thought that was the end of the experience.

Not a Touch, but a Transformation

Since I felt normal again, I went downstairs to explain to my in-laws what had happened. Before I could explain, my mother-in-law set a plate of food before me and said, "Isn't the Lord wonderful?" And when she said that, I could feel the glory of the Lord coming upon me again. I fell backwards to the floor and began shaking. Then I began to crawl up the stairs again to my bedroom.

I was supposed to confirm with another pastor in the area that I would preach in his church, but I could not even make a phone call. I was thinking, *Lord, if this fire is from You, how come I am not doing Your work? I should be busy—busier than ever before.* I had an impressive to-do list sitting on top of my desk in my bedroom. Also, the airplane ticket for the trip was expensive, so I felt I had to get things done. I looked at that list and the list looked at me, and I wanted to get busy for the Lord. But the Lord had different plans for me. He did not regard my agenda—He ripped it to pieces!

That night I went to a service where several congregations were meeting together. I sat in the back, and suddenly the presence of the Lord came on strong and the uncontrollable trembling with it.

I said to myself, *I do not know what these people will think if this manifestation starts again.* So I ran to my car and continued to shake as I drove all the way from one city to another. I just wanted to get back to my in-laws' home again and hide there.

The Lord did not regard my agenda—
He ripped it to pieces!

The next day, the presence of the Lord was even more powerful than on Sunday. At 7:00 A.M. I began to iron my shirt; I wanted to leave the house and do things for God. I did not finish ironing my shirt until about 3:00 P.M., because as I was ironing, the glory of the Lord would fill the room and I would fall on the floor and worship Him.

HIS MANIFEST PRESENCE

God is not equal to us—He is more powerful. That is why He cannot fit into our old patterns. That is why you cannot have an outpouring of His Spirit in your life and keep the same old wineskins. We must have a change of wineskins before the Spirit can descend. If you are so taken with your own ways and patterns and the Holy Spirit comes, He will break the old wineskins.

But new wineskins are different because they stretch. The Lord will impart to many of you a flexibility for the Holy Spirit. You will say, "Lord, I can stretch; it does not matter that I am more than forty or fifty or sixty. There is room in my heart for your will."

Matthew 3:11 says, "He will baptize you with the Holy Spirit and with fire." So many people say, "Oh, I received the Holy Spirit fifteen years ago." I believe that the Holy Spirit comes to our hearts when we receive Jesus. That is the beginning. His presence is with us. We could not be Christians without the Holy Spirit. But then comes the baptism of the Holy Spirit. When we receive Christ, the Spirit comes to dwell within us. When we are baptized by the Spirit, the Spirit overflows through us. Different external signs may occur as God designates them. But the sure inner evidence is the power to witness (see Acts 1:8) and renewed passion for God and souls.

Somehow we have managed to divide the baptism of the Holy Spirit from the fire of the Holy Spirit. We must remember the words of John the Baptist, who did not divide the two but said that Jesus would baptize us with the Holy Spirit *and* with fire. The two go hand-in-hand. We are meant to do great exploits for God and to live lives of holy passion.

Many Christians do not produce fruit because they say, "I have the Holy Spirit, but I don't have the fire. I don't have the fire for the nations, for my city or for my lost relatives." He is moving in power like never before, and manifesting Himself through miraculous signs and wonders. I believe the Holy Spirit is the same today, tomorrow and yesterday, but He can choose how He manifests His presence to His people. He can manifest His presence through a beautiful anointed river, but He can also manifest His presence through an abrupt fire of God. He is in the earthquake, and He is in the breeze.

The anointing is sweet, and can be described as God's deposit of gifts and grace within us. It is a tangible presence of God to do ministry. But the fire is abrupt; it will consume all you have! The fire adds fuel to the anointing and empowers us to even greater levels of holiness. The fire equips; the anointing empowers.

It is up to Him how He chooses to manifest Himself, but the Lord is dealing with the Church in stronger ways in these days. The Bride of Jesus Christ is almost ready for the Bridegroom. The Holy Spirit is ironing out the last few wrinkles and cleaning the few remaining spots and making the Church beautiful for that great wedding between His Church and our Lord and Savior Jesus Christ!

Are you ready for the Holy Spirit to interrupt your agenda and do what He wants? Sometimes we say, "Lord, change my life, but do not change my formalism. Do not touch my safe ground. This is my area and I do not want You to get too close." But when you pray for revival, the problem is that sometimes you get it!

The Lord wants to descend in power upon every person. Everyone. But we must allow the Holy Spirit to do His work, in His way and in His timing, because the Lord God Almighty is sovereign.

2

THE FEAR OF
THE LORD

I sensed waves of the Holy Spirit flowing over my life those first two days that I was under this fire of the Lord. But my mind was not changed until the third day. That day, everything changed. I woke up and there was a sadness in my room. The same beautiful presence of God that was loving me and hugging me the day before was now rejecting me and coming too strong. God's presence seemed dangerously close to me.

That morning, the holiness of God was so close and so strong in my room that I became very scared and I began to back up. I backed up until my back touched the wall. Then I thought, *What am I doing? This is a spiritual presence of the Lord. I cannot hide from it.* I began to pray, "Please Lord, no more." It was the first time I had ever prayed in such a way. I was so scared I said, "Lord, I don't think I can take any more. You are too holy."

Sometimes when we are at a distance from Jesus Christ, we become comfortable with our lifestyle. But when Jesus gets very close to us, we become uncomfortable. Maybe even as you read this book, you may become uncomfortable. You may think, *What is happening to me?* Reader, let me assure you that the holiness of the Lord can descend upon you. His presence and fire is real. When He gets close to His people, something changes dramatically. We cannot enter the holy place of God without being transformed.

So I said, "Lord, what is it? I know there is something wrong. Please have mercy on me. Don't kill me here." But God did not answer me then.

That afternoon I went for a walk around my in-laws' property. As I was walking down a gravel path, the power of God came over me very suddenly and threw me to my knees. It was so sudden and unpredictable that immediately I broke down in tears. Then the Holy Spirit began to show me pictures of sin in my life. He showed me areas where sin had crept in and remained unresolved.

I was born and raised in a Christian home and even as an infant, my parents used to read the Bible to me. My parents raised me in the ways of the Lord. But now God was dealing with what I had thought were "evangelical sins," small things—things the Church seemed to wink at and say, "Well, it's OK if you lust a little or covet a little. Just make sure you do not let it get out of hand." I had accepted a distortion of biblical teaching that it is OK if we always have a percentage of sin or evil in us. But now the Holy Spirit was resisting me. He was not hugging me.

TIME DOES NOT ERASE SIN

While I was there on the gravel path, the Lord pointed out specific things in my life that were not right. I thought time would erase these sins because they were so minor. But I was reminded that little sin is still sin. All sin is evil and destructive. I saw flashes of a time when I had hardened my heart against a brother. I could see the very place where it had happened. I had never mistreated him, but I had made a silent pledge to never get close to him again. I was reminded of times when my eyes had lingered too long on images that were not pleasing to the Lord.

I began to weep for my sin and felt such a pain for my wrong-doings that I felt sick, as if a fever were coming over my body. The Holy Spirit began to speak to me and now my mind began to catch up with what the Lord was trying to do. He said, "Because you are neither cold nor hot, I will spit you out of My mouth." I was shocked. "Lord," I responded, "I have been in the ministry for years; I am a preacher of Your Word. I fasted last week and I pray every day. How have I been so deceived? Why have I never seen this before?"

98% HOLINESS IS NOT ENOUGH

The Lord said to me, "I wish you would be as cold as a pagan, so I could save you again, or as hot as a believer that has given 100% to Me. Then I could use you in My own way." Then He repeated this stern warning to me: "Because you are neither hot nor cold, I will spit you out of My mouth." Then the Lord answered my question about why I had not seen this before. He said, "Deceitful is the heart of man, and desperately wicked." I was terrified. I could not believe that God was speaking these things to me. Then the Lord spoke to me again and said clearly, *"98% holiness is not enough."*

Sometime after these events, I was reading a magazine article about leukemia. It said that the disease starts with a genetic change in *a single white blood cell* in the bone marrow. That disease we pray against and go to hospitals to be healed from—that disease begins with a genetic change in a single white blood cell. And, my friends, that is the way sin operates in our lives—even in the life of a minister, a servant of God. He has a genetic change, a spiritual change in his heart. Maybe a little lust, maybe a little envy, maybe just a small lie. Maybe the sin is some hatred against someone in his church who is making his life impossible. That is enough to pollute the entire system. Then we cannot say as the apostle Paul said, "My conscience is clear" (1 Cor. 4:4).

Many believers have experienced only the blessings of the Lord up to this point in their lives. And His blessings are wonderful. But in order to be used mightily by Him, we must also be cleansed. The same Lord that loves us and blesses us is coming to do surgery in our hearts. We cannot be in the ministry and have evil habits in our private lives. Some have said, "Well then, I will get out of the ministry." No! Get the evil habits out of your heart!

In a sense, I was a Pharisee of Pharisees. My goal was to be fairly holy, to do fairly well, to pass the examination with an 80%. But the Lord had different demands. He rebuked me for my self-righteousness and exposed the lie of my heart. I then realized my greatest error: I was not trying to be like Jesus. I was just trying to be fairly good.

At that moment I felt that all my religiosity and discipline was like filthy rags in His presence. I realized I had not believed that the Lord had called me to be like Jesus. I had wrongly believed that He had called me to be a fairly good person. The week before my trip to the States I had fasted one day and prayed a lot and felt good about myself. I felt I must have been at least 90% holy.

Sometimes we let apparently insignificant sins lodge themselves in our hearts. But let me ask you this question: What percentage of evil do you think He will allow us to take with us when the day of the Lord comes? By faith, we must allow Him to cleanse us.

As I was still kneeling on the gravel path, God continued speaking to me in terms that even a child could understand. At the time, I would have been unable to understand anything very complex. He told me, "Nobody gets up in the morning and prepares a cup of coffee, puts just one drop of poison in it,

No one would buy water labeled
"98% Pure Mineral Water, 2% Sewage Water."

then stirs and drinks it." He revealed that many people in the Church allow poison into their hearts and minds. Without a doubt, this small quota of daily sin is destroying them. No one would consider buying a bottle of mineral water with a label that reads: "98% Pure Mineral Water, 2% Sewage Water." Yet many Christians have allowed spiritual sewage water to seep into their lives.

So many people wonder, *Why do I lose the strength of the Lord so quickly? Maybe it is because I am a failure, or maybe it is because I am not trained.* I tell you that when there is sin in even 1% of our hearts, it can eventually destroy every ounce of devotion in our lives.

CONVICTION OF SIN, NOT GUILT

I wept, I confessed and I repented. The Lord pointed out to me specific sins in my life; He did not just point out generalities. Satan has a fake ministry that he uses especially in the Church.

His ministry is a ministry of bringing guilt. The Bible tells us that Satan is the accuser of the brethren (see Rev. 12:10). He comes to put a general sense of guilt into our hearts and minds, but never helps us to resolve such guilt. Then all we do is feel bad. Some leaders, workers and servants of the Lord are trying their best, but they are tortured by guilt. Before they preach they have to get rid of the guilt for one hour, and then it comes back to them. That is not the ministry of the Holy Spirit.

The ministry of the Holy Spirit is to bring conviction of sin (see John 16:8). God speaks very directly and specifically and His Word is very clear. He tells us what is wrong with our hearts, our thoughts and our affections and demands repentance from us. If we listen to His voice, He will change us. That is the work of the Holy Spirit (see 2 Cor. 7:10).

It is very different from the work of Satan, who comes to destroy lives and pull entire ministries into depression and loneliness. There are people who think, *I hope nobody will find out the way I am in private.* Dear servant of the Lord, when the fire of the Holy Spirit comes upon you, you will say with the apostle Paul, "My conscience is clean" (1 Cor. 4:4). Your life will be purified because of Jesus.

On that third day, May 20, I gradually began to recover the joy of the Lord. But now instead of landing in the same place of fear, I had changed to a new address. The joy of the Lord was in that room. The same glory from the day before returned. For six days I was in the presence of almighty God, weeping and crying. When I thought I was normal, I would put on my tie and jacket and get ready to do some business for God. But before I could touch the doorknob, the power of God would come upon me and throw me to the floor. At times I would be there for hours before I could get up.

SURRENDERING THE GOOD FOR THE BEST

Two weeks later I was preparing to return to my congregation in La Plata. Just before leaving the States to return to Argentina, I attended a pastors' prayer meeting. A pastor friend of mine was present, and I said to him, "I am returning to Argentina now; I would like to have your phone number and I will give you mine." He was writing my phone number in his address book and I noticed it began to shake. I asked him, "Are you receiving the same thing that I received?" That was the end of the conversation.

Right there in the church parking lot he fell to the ground under the power of God. There was a Christian school next door, and I could see the parents dropping off their kids and looking at this fellow lying on the ground. I thought, *I cannot let this guy affect me too much, because we are in a parking lot*. But the power of God came upon me, and I also fell to the ground.

Two other pastors came out of the church and rushed over to where we were, thinking there had been an accident. As they approached us they said, "The Lord is here—this is holy ground," and they took off their shoes. They fell under the power of God and began to praise God and prophesy. We stayed there for hours. The anointing was so strong that others had to carry us to our cars and drive us to our homes.

The pastor with the address book shook so hard that his university graduation ring fell off his hand. When he picked it up he raised it and said, "Lord, now I know that You not only take evil out of my life, but that You take even good things away from me to give me the best." Then he did the same thing with his wallet, his keys, everything he had. He said, "I give You my ministry and my life. Nothing is mine; I give everything to You."

Today this pastor is a personal friend and I can say that his life and ministry have dramatically changed since that encounter in the parking lot.

GOD WON'T CHANGE HIS MIND ABOUT YOU

I share my testimony not just to tell you about something that is happening on the other side of the world. The Lord has directed me to impart to you what He has given to me. Silver and gold we have none, but what we have we give to you in the name of Jesus (see Acts 3:6). You can receive the fire of God.

I want to speak a word of faith to many of you: The Lord does not change His mind. He does not come to you today and then tomorrow say, "Sorry, you were the wrong guy." He loves you and what He wants to give you is forever, until Jesus returns. You see, if we pursue purity and remain in Him each day, the fire of God is inextinguishable.

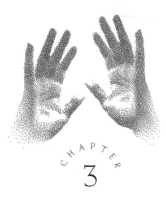

LIVING CLOSE TO THE FLAMES: REVIVAL IN ARGENTINA

To understand how the fire of God works in a person and a nation, I would like to tell you about the revival in Argentina. This will give you some background for the testimony of the fire that came into my life, as I shared in the first two chapters.

Many good books have been written about the revivals in Argentina. I will tell the story, however, from my own personal experience and the experiences told by my parents, Rev. and Mrs. Alberto Scataglini, as they lived it firsthand.

TOMMY HICKS COMES TO ARGENTINA

The first great Christian revival most talked about in Argentina occurred between 1954 and 1957, when Tommy Hicks, an American evangelist, conducted several campaigns. During the time he was in Argentina, he began challenging pastors to believe in greater things from God. And greater things began happening.

During his visit to Argentina in 1954 and 1955, Hicks filled the largest stadiums in the country. According to firsthand accounts (including the testimony of my parents), more than 100,000 people attended some of these crusades. Several thousands more lined up outside the stadiums, only to be turned away. I grew up hearing stories about the traffic congestion, subway jams and rerouting of city buses due to the overwhelming number of people who attended these historic events. Thousands of people received miraculous healings and tens of thousands more were saved in those great crusades. For the first time, the Bible Society in Argentina ran out of Bibles because of the high demand.

I was born in March 1957. Hicks returned to Argentina one last time a few months after I was born. One of my parents' greatest keepsakes from that time is a picture of Tommy Hicks holding me up for the camera, as he blessed me and prayed that I would be a servant of the Lord.

Despite the mass salvations and healings, after just a few years the evangelical churches in Argentina settled back into a "normal" maintenance mode (by "evangelical" I am referring to all born-again Christians). From the early '60s until the mid-1980s, the church growth rate in Argentina was one of the slowest in the world. And then came Carlos Annacondia.

ANNACONDIA COMES TO TOWN

In the early 1980s, my father's church in La Plata, now called Puerta del Cielo (Doorway to Heaven), of which I am now senior pastor, began praying for a great harvest. The youth spent many evenings in all-night prayer meetings. A prophetic word was given to the church during that time that an *avalanche* of people was coming and that they should prepare for it. My father told the congregation, "Those of you who have been around here for many years better hang on to your seats. Because when the avalanche of new people comes, you will not have a place to sit." Little did he realize just how soon those words would come true.

After finishing Bible school at the Instituto Biblico Rio de la Plata in Lomas de Zamora, Argentina, in 1978, I went for a year of study to Eastern Pentecostal Bible College in Ontario, Canada, where I received a certificate from their Special Bible Studies program. I then attended Southern California Bible College and graduated with a B.A. in religion. I returned to Argentina and I and a brother founded a church in downtown Buenos Aires. Shortly thereafter, the brother left and I took over as the sole pastor. What I thought was going to be a four-month stay in Argentina turned into four years as I pastored in Buenos Aires.

After that time, I felt the Lord leading me to return to continue my studies at Fuller Theological Seminary in Pasadena, California. So in the fall of 1983, I once again left Argentina for North America. I would eventually earn my M.A. in theology and missions from Fuller (in 1986).

In March 1984, while I was at Fuller, my father decided to take a few days of rest with my family, and we retreated to a small cabin on the outskirts of town. While there, a pastor named Pablo Terechovich drove out to the cabin to talk to my father. With urgency in his voice he said, "Won't you please return to the city to support the citywide campaign we are planning? We would like your church to be involved."

Alberto asked, "Who is going to be the speaker?"

Pastor Pablo replied, "A brother named Carlos Annacondia. He is an evangelist."

Because Carlos Annacondia was unknown to the pastors, Alberto agreed to return to the city. My father was anxious to meet with this evangelist to see who he was and what he was all about. My father was seated across from this new evangelist and began asking the obvious questions. He asked Annacondia about the church he came from, how his ministry began and what the Lord had been doing in his life. While he listened to Annacondia, he was praying in his spirit and listening to what the Holy Spirit was saying.

The Lord was preparing something completely new for the Church in Argentina.

While Annacondia was responding to his questions, the Holy Spirit said to Alberto, "This is My servant; I have sent him. Listen to what he says." Alberto stopped the conversation right then and there and said, "Brother Carlos, say no more. Come and minister in the campaign; from now on you will be an Elijah, and I will be an Elisha. I will do whatever you say. I will follow what the Lord is doing in you. The Lord gave you the vision; my part is to obey and follow you."

Annacondia felt very uncomfortable—and said so—that an older, respected pastor would offer to follow him, especially since Annacondia had only been a Christian for a few years. But that is the way the Lord would have it, as He was preparing something completely new for the Church in Argentina.

REVIVAL STARTS IN LA PLATA

Rev. Alberto Scataglini recounts the story of how the Lord brought revival to Argentina:

> It seemed that for every new thing the Lord did in the revival, an old structure was destroyed. This was how the Lord began preparing the minds and hearts of the Christians for the new things they were about to experience.
>
> After hearing from the Lord to accept and support this new and unknown evangelist, I was in shock when Annacondia and his team members said, "Great! We will begin the campaign in two weeks." Two weeks?! It takes six months to plan a campaign, prepare the workers, rent a site and set up the grounds. That was the first old structure to be destroyed.
>
> The following week, I (Alberto) accompanied Annacondia and his helper, Juan Dicresensio, to find a place to hold the campaign in the city of La Plata. We drove around looking at empty lots that might be suitable for an open-air campaign, and Carlos and Juan finally felt they had found the ideal spot. They both sensed strong confirmation from the Lord and began a search to find the owners.
>
> After locating the owners of the lot, however, the owners were very strong in their answer and said there was absolutely no way they would give permission. I wanted to continue looking, but Juan said, "We have to keep insisting; they said no, but the Lord said yes." After revisiting the owners several times and after much prayer, [Carlos and Juan] finally got the yes they were

waiting for. Preparations began immediately as the campaign was to begin the following week.

The first night of the evangelistic meetings was something completely different from what we were used to. When we arrived we saw some poles, a few strings of lights, a few chairs, some rope surrounding the grounds and a tent that the evangelistic team had erected. We said to ourselves, *No one will show up here.* We felt a little bit embarrassed.

The tent was to be used to minister to those with spiritual problems. It later became known as the Intensive Care Tent. The meetings themselves were held outside under a few strands of lights. When the meeting started, Annacondia's worship leader began to lead the singing. It certainly was not the music and hymns we were used to singing. It was more like old time country music with blue-grass choruses. We did not know what to think, until Annacondia arrived and began preaching.

His preaching was very Christ-centered, and we were thrilled. After preaching a powerful message about Christ, we were surprised when he said, "Listen to me Satan, hear me well," and began to rebuke the devil and command him to leave that place and the lives of the people there. When the service was all said and done, 140 people gave their lives to Christ that first night! That was a miracle for Argentina, which at that time had one of the slowest church growth rates in the world. Yet still we were not prepared for what was to come.

During the campaign, people would bring the clothing of their sick relatives to be prayed over. Tables were piled high with those pieces of clothing. One testimony that stands out in my mind was of a woman who brought a pair of her husband's socks to be prayed for; he was unable to walk. She took them home and the following day her husband put them on. All of a sudden he began screaming that the socks were burning his feet and he began jumping up and down. It took him a few moments to realize that he was able to jump! He had been healed.

There were so many things that happened during the campaign with Annacondia in La Plata in 1984. It completely changed our lives and our church. We learned more about God and the spiritual world than we had learned in all the previous years put together of studying theology and pastoring churches.

We read about the Ark of the Covenant in the Old Testament and how something physical happened to those who touched it (they dropped dead!). Something similar happened to those who came to the Annacondia campaign. As people stepped onto the lot where the meetings were being held, many with spiritual problems fell to the ground as if they had fainted and others manifested demons.

We (a few pastors) arrived at the campaign tents at 5:00 P.M. to provide pastoral help and counseling for anyone who desired it. People were open to spiritual things and came to see us with many problems. Many times I remember sitting at the table where I was doing pastoral counseling and having to run out and pray for someone who had just fallen to the ground as they stepped onto the lot. We counseled and prayed for people from the time we arrived until the meeting was over. We usually left the tent around 2:00 or 3:00 A.M.

There was a spiritual revolution in the air. The battle did not end when we turned out the lights. We would arrive at our homes sometime after three in the morning. We could not sleep right away, talking and sharing about the wonders and miracles we had seen. But many times people would knock at our doors at 3:00 or 4:00 A.M., wanting us to pray for them or some family member who needed deliverance from demonic spirits. Not only did people manifest demons when they came to the campaigns, but many times after they arrived back at their homes.

It got to the point where we would sleep in our clothes. We would just lay on top of our beds, fully dressed, until the next person would come. For two full years we did not rest adequately one single day. We were preaching every day and opening new preaching points in the city to take care of the people who had come to the Lord. We were providing pastoral counseling for those who needed help. It is wonderful to pray and believe for a revival, but it is equally important to be willing to pay the price for revival when it happens.

When the Annacondia campaign was over, the new people who had been converted would line up for two blocks just to get into the church building at service time. All of our carefully laid plans and church activities were blown away. Our church has never been the same. More than 50,000 people came to the Lord in La Plata during the six-month campaign with Carlos Annacondia in 1984. Many of them form a great part of the church body today in La Plata.

Although many wonderful things were happening in our city, and many new people were added to the church, not everyone was happy about the revival—namely some of the older Christians. Some were upset because they had literally "lost their seats" in the church. The churches were invaded by many of the new people that had come to the Lord during the campaign. (The reaction was similar to that of an older sibling when a new baby joins the family!) Some would say, "We have lost our pastor."

Despite the cold, rain and mud at times, services were held every night for six months. When the La Plata campaign was over, I was asked to be the forerunner for Annacondia in other cities in which he was planning campaigns. My task was to hold talks with the pastors of those cities to prepare them for the coming campaign.

The main concept I wanted the pastors to understand was that the campaign was going to be like no other crusade or revival meeting they had ever experienced. The difference was that this campaign would change the very structure of their churches. The main change would be less intervention of man and more intervention of the Holy Spirit in their services. That was not because what they were doing before was bad, but rather that the Church was going to move to another level of glory. It was basically a change from one way of life to another.

DARE TO MAKE YOURSELF AVAILABLE

At the time all of this was happening, I was studying at Fuller Seminary, taking church growth courses with Dr. C. Peter Wagner. Both Dr. Wagner and my classmates were very interested in the development of the move of God in Argentina. At times I would read aloud to the class the letters I was receiving from La Plata with incredible news about this new move of God.

Fellow students often asked me what was the key to having such an incredible outpouring. I called my father in La Plata and asked him the same question. My father simply responded, "I believe the key is availability. We did not hinder the work of the Spirit, but made ourselves available to God."

Dear brother and sister, even to this day we are feeling the aftershocks of those first campaigns. Since that time, other new waves of power have visited Argentina. The key remains the same: availability.

Would you dare to become available to the Holy Spirit no matter what—in success or persecution? For a long ministry or for a shorter life? Do you hunger for revival and salvation of souls to such an extent that you would say, "Lord, I am available to You!"? If so, take a moment and write a note to the Lord or pray out loud something like this:

Dear Lord,

I am willing to pay the price. I am available to be used of You.

My love for You cancels my fear of the unknown. Your love in me for the lost cancels my selfishness and self-gratification. I withhold nothing from You. Make me an instrument of revival.

100% Yours,

*X*_____

ANOINTED FOR
HOLINESS

When the Argentine revival began in 1984 with Annacondia, I was at Fuller Seminary in Pasadena, California, missing out on most of the initial excitement. At first, I could only imagine the revival from the newspaper clippings and exciting letters I was receiving from my parents. I quickly shared them with my professor of Church Growth, Dr. C. Peter Wagner. In late 1985, I finally took a trimester off at Fuller and returned to see the revival firsthand.

During my break from Fuller, I spent time in my hometown of La Plata. It was very apparent to me that Annacondia and his campaigns were changing the spiritual atmosphere of Argentina. It is said that he has led more than two million people to the Lord since 1984. Churches that had been experiencing no growth now had a new influx of people who had been saved in his campaigns. The way most congregations "did church" had changed. In general, there was more openness to the moving of the Holy Spirit and to new things of the Spirit.

In the spring of 1986, I returned to Fuller, where I had by now met Kathy, my future wife, who was also a student. We were married in Elkhart, Indiana, in July 1986. We continued to live in Pasadena, as Kathy was finishing her master's at Fuller as well. A year later we founded Scataglini Ministries, Inc., and in December 1987, we were "sent out" to Argentina. Our goal was to work with my father's church to establish a school, an orphanage and a leadership training program. By the end of 1990, the school and orphanage had been established and the leadership training program was already implemented. Kathy and I then felt the Lord calling us to move back to the States.

We moved to Elkhart in October 1990 and established Prayer Partners Ministry. Its main purpose was to unite Christians in prayer for revival. During that time, I also began taping Moments of Prayer, which were radio spots leading listeners in prayer for revival; they aired for seven years on Christian radio.

REVIVAL FROM AFAR—AGAIN

While living in Elkhart, Indiana, we began hearing about new things that God was doing in Argentina through Pastor Claudio Freidzon. When I began hearing reports from my friends, it really caught my attention because Claudio had been one of my roommates in Bible college at Instituto Biblico Rio de la Plata! I had always known Claudio to be a quiet person, but the stories we were hearing spoke of stadiums being filled and Claudio ministering powerfully with a great anointing. These descriptions were totally out of character for this unassuming man. I knew it must be the work of the Holy Spirit.

One day I called Claudio at his home in Buenos Aires. I said, "Claudio, what is going on? Tell me." Claudio confirmed the reports I had been hearing. As he was telling me about the things the Lord was doing, my heart became so much more hungry for revival. I felt acutely needy at that point. I tried to hide my true state, because it would have been embarrassing to reveal just how desperate I was to receive from God. During the following months, I spent many hours a day in prayer, desiring more of God in my life. I was at a point of spiritual despair.

Sometime later, in 1993, we found out that Claudio was going to be in Cincinnati, Ohio, attending a large crusade of another evangelist. We decided to make the trip from Elkhart to Cincinnati to see Claudio, about 200 miles away. I had only one goal in mind: I was going there to see him, because he had received an anointing from the Holy Spirit and I wanted Claudio to pray for me!

I arrived at the large stadium in Cincinnati to find thousands of people staking out seats; the arena was filled to capacity. Claudio had told me that he would save a seat for me in the front row. I slowly made my way down front as the worship began. I was excited to spot Claudio; he was waiting for me and sure enough had saved a seat. My goal was that this man, after this conference, would pray for me. I had driven three and a half hours for that purpose and nothing else.

When I sat down, one of the ushers came and said, "Sir, this seat is reserved, you must go to the back." I knew there was no more room in the whole stadium and that I would have to sit somewhere "way back there." If I moved, I knew I would lose sight of Claudio. He was becoming well known and it was hard to get prayed for by him.

I began to pray while the usher was talking to Claudio. I was praying silently, *God, I need to be in this place. Please arrange it somehow.*

Then someone from the second row said, "I have been in these meetings several times already. You can have my seat, and I will sit somewhere else."

I thanked God for that, but I had this sense that somehow I was in the wrong place. It was hard. I almost had to fight for my seat! And then I said to my friend, "Claudio, would you pray for me?"

He said, "Well, when the meeting is over, I will pray for you."

I enjoyed the presence of the Lord during the event, but I kept dwelling on the fact that Claudio was going to pray for me after the meeting. When the meeting was over, however, he said, "I have a scheduled dinner with the evangelist of this crusade, so I might not be able to pray for you tonight."

I did not know what was going on. I now believe God was testing me, but at the time I was getting a little impatient. After the meeting, Claudio asked if I wanted to wait for him while he went to confirm his dinner appointment. Perhaps something had come up and the evangelist would not be able to meet him. Claudio would then be able to go out with me. I was happy to wait, knowing there was a possibility I could spend time with him.

I waited 10 minutes, 15 minutes, 20 minutes—the stadium was totally empty. When an endless half hour had gone by, I thought, *Am I the only fool standing here with a Bible under his arm waiting for this man to come and pray for him? How foolish I am to have stayed here so long, waiting for nothing. Why did I drive so many hours to come to this place? What is going on here? Lord, I am hungry for You. Lord, I need You.*

I thought my friend had probably forgotten about me. Just as I was thinking these things, Claudio returned to the stage area and said, "Let's go for dinner." My heart rejoiced at the opportunity. I believe if he would have asked me to go play tennis, I would have done it, too! I would have done anything, just as long as he prayed for me.

I WOULD NOT GIVE UP

At the restaurant, I could hardly wait for the break between dinner and dessert so Claudio could pray for me. So I asked him, "Claudio, will you pray for me now?"

He said, "Not here. Let's go back to my hotel room later on." I agreed.

We went to his hotel room and he gave me some videos of the crusades he had been holding in Argentina. It was about 2:30 A.M. by this time, and I kept waiting for that prayer. Finally I had the chance to ask him, "Now, Claudio, will you pray for me?"

He answered, "Why don't you come to one of my crusades in Argentina and I will pray for you."

By this time I was desperate. I said, "I cannot go to Argentina right now." I did not say it, but I knew I could not wait that long. I insisted so much that my friend and brother finally prayed for me. The Lord knew what He was doing. Claudio prayed a simple prayer over my life, and I left.

God reached inside of me and removed the pain of loneliness and depression.

When I left that place, I was not sure anything had happened except that I felt a deep peace. But that was all. The next day, Kathy and I and our three young boys—Nathan, Jeremy and Miqueas (then four, three and a few months old)—headed home to Elkhart. On our drive back to Indiana, the kids were very restless. I thought that the little anointing I had received would be lost.

But I did not know that the Holy Spirit had come upon me and had already answered my prayer. Although I had been born in a Christian home, up to that time I did not know anything about the anointing. Looking back now, I realize that the Lord had been testing my faith. It was not that Claudio did not want to pray for me but, rather, that the Lord Himself was holding back in silence. It almost appeared like a rejection because He was seeing if I really wanted to receive His anointing. I received it!

The next day I began to experience a new freedom in my heart—an inner healing had taken place. I felt that God had reached His hand inside of me and removed what was still left of the pain of loneliness and depression that I had experienced in the past. For the next four years, I was able to preach with a freedom and new anointing that before that time I had seen only sporadically. I dwelled in the anointing. The receptivity to the Holy Spirit I gained with the anointing paved the way for me to receive, four years later, another blessing in a stronger way—the baptism of fire.

Kathy, our boys and I moved back to Argentina in March 1994 after a season of ministry in Elkhart and began working with my father on the pastoral staff at Puerta del Cielo. In December 1996, I was installed as senior pastor; my father stayed on as a key part of the pastoral team. We had a constant moving of the Holy Spirit in our services. Souls were being saved on a regular basis, yet in prayer I found myself crying out to God for more of Him and for a revival in our midst.

Soon afterward, I made my unforgettable trip to the States that forever changed my life.

C H A P T E R

5

A FRESH MANIFESTATION OF THE FIRE OF GOD

A s I recounted in chapters 1 and 2, God changed my life forever in May 1997. Several weeks later, I was finally ready to return to Argentina. Before I returned to La Plata, I had already mentally prepared a speech. I knew what I was going to tell my people so that they would not be scared of this new fire of God. They had already heard different versions. I was determined in my mind that the church would not divide over something like this.

Upon my return to the pulpit during a midweek service, revival took over in the first five minutes. As I arrived at the church, walked to the platform and took the microphone, God immediately threw me on the floor. Some of my friends had the bright idea to remove the pulpit and flowers from the platform so that the people could see me shaking on the floor.

I said to an associate pastor, "Please go get Claudio Freidzon; he is across the street in my car." Claudio had come to La Plata so we could spend the day together in prayer. I had asked him if he would come and minister to my people that evening. Claudio, seeing the new fire in my life, declined but said he would like to sit and hear me minister. I said, "How can I minister with a man of God like you sitting there? I can't." So we agreed that because the hour was late, I would go in and greet the congregation, give my little speech of explanation and invite them all to Sunday service. Claudio was to wait outside.

The pastor nodded at me, but he did not move. He thought I was seeing a vision or something. It would be very unusual for Claudio to be out in the car while we were having service inside. I said, "Go get him." My associate finally believed me and went to get Claudio. By the time he showed up on the platform, the whole church was on their knees or on the floor, crying out in repentance. Many people began asking forgiveness of each other. The meeting went on for hours.

After that meeting, we saw the beginning of a revival in our church. Ever since June 1997, many new people have come to Christ, and a spirit of repentance and recommitment has swept through our congregation. Thankfully, I have not been the only Argentine pastor to receive this touch from God. Many churches and pastors throughout Argentina have been experiencing a fresh wind and power of His presence. This fire of holiness is serving to fan the flames of revival again in Argentina.

WATER ON THE SACRIFICE

My brother and sister, I am not suggesting that you have to tremble on the floor to experience revival fire. The Lord chooses

His signs and wonders as He wants. But I do affirm that God is seeking people who will say, "Lord, take everything from me. I give myself to You 100%." This fire of holiness will purify you. This fire of holiness can shorten your life. Some of you are looking for longevity, comfort, larger incomes or bigger ministries. Are you ready to surrender these things to His will?

I might as well tell you right now: When Elijah prepared for the fire of God to come, he not only deposited the offering and the wood, he also threw 12 jars of water on it (see 1 Kings 18:33,34). I want to throw some water on the sacrifice right now so that you *know* that the fire that comes from the Holy Spirit is genuine.

Some of you have been seeking the Holy Spirit for years, but for the wrong reasons. You want personal aggrandizement; you are full of personal ambition. If you are a pastor, maybe you just want to see your ministry grow. But you will never be happy until you surrender all your ambitions to Jesus Christ. Then the fire will come and you will be the happiest person on earth with the true joy of the Holy Spirit.

GOD DOES NOT SKIP THE MINISTERS

A few days after my return to Argentina, I attended a meeting with the pastors in La Plata. They all came together for an Argentine-style barbecue and asked me to share my testimony. I was concerned about how they would receive it, and I asked the Lord to keep them from being offended. As I was sharing the testimony, one of the pastors began to scream. He screamed so loud that I forgot what I was saying. He was screaming because he felt a fire burning in him for his sins.

I suggested we all pray, and the power of God descended very strongly upon the pastors. I have never seen anything like it.

Some of them actually fell out of their chairs headfirst onto the floor. The rest knelt down or put their faces to the floor as the conviction of the Holy Spirit fell upon them. I am not talking about a warm, carpeted floor. We were in a concrete building with a concrete floor, on a chilly Argentine winter day.

Before I arrived, the pastors had planned a debriefing session for afterward to discuss this fire of the Lord. When they finished praying that day, one of the pastors stood up and said, "How do we dare discuss this; this is of God." The other pastors agreed, but decided that they would get together again that night at 11:00. Even more pastors came at night and the same glory of the Lord descended upon that place.

FIRE PLEASE, HOLD THE MIRACLES

Some people ask, Can we have the fire of God without all of these strange signs and wonders? I do not know, but I can tell you this: Signs and wonders are strange, divine things that point the attention of the people to the Lord Jesus Christ. If the sign captures a person's attention and directs them to Jesus Christ, then we say "Welcome" to the sign:

> When the crowds heard Philip and saw the miraculous signs he did, they all paid close attention to what he said (Acts 8:6).

The miraculous rapidly advances the gospel:

> I will not venture to speak of anything except what Christ has accomplished through me in leading the Gentiles to obey God by what I have said and done—by the power of signs and miracles, through the power of the Spirit. So

from Jerusalem all the way around to Illyricum, I have
fully proclaimed the gospel of Christ (Rom. 15:18,19).

Signs do not discredit the ministry. Signs can add credibility to it:

> Men of Israel, listen to this: Jesus of Nazareth was a man
> *accredited* by God to you by miracles, wonders and signs,
> which God did among you through him, as you yourselves
> know (Acts 2:22; emphasis mine).

> Then the disciples went out and preached everywhere,
> and the Lord worked with them and confirmed his word
> by the signs that accompanied it (Mark 16:20).

This new wave of holiness takes on strength when it is marked
by miraculous signs such as healing, shaking and sometimes,
deliverance from the demonic. My ministry is primarily the
preaching of a message of holiness, but these signs often follow.
Some people have experienced physical healing even as they came
forward to repent, without any mention of healing and without
being prayed for.

COUNTERFEITS OF HOLINESS

In order for us to move forward in holiness, we must be aware of
the counterfeits the enemy uses to steal and destroy. Here is a
list, though I have not covered every possible example.

Legalism

Many Christians are afraid to pursue purity because they fear
falling into legalism. Some have experienced religious trauma
from those who preach holiness as a laborious list of do's and

don'ts. They belong to the group that Paul warns against in Colossians 2:20,21:

> Since you died with Christ to the basic principles of this world, why, as though you still belonged to it, do you submit to its rules: "Do not handle! Do not taste! Do not touch!"

Remember, holiness is not a list but a person: Jesus Christ. He has become our righteousness and sanctification (see 1 Cor. 1:30). Legalism believes salvation is by faith but that sanctification is by works. But the reality is that both salvation and sanctification are by faith accompanied by repentance and obedience.

Human Perfectionism

Human effort and self-discipline have the appearance of holiness, but are far from it. Even though self-discipline is necessary in our lives, it will not produce holiness. Some may think that purity is attained by attending to every vain detail—it becomes a religious trivial pursuit. The experts of the law in Jesus' time were like this. Jesus rebuked them sternly:

> Woe to you, teachers of the law and Pharisees, you hypocrites! You give a tenth of your spices—mint, dill and cummin. But you have neglected the more important matters of the law—justice, mercy and faithfulness. You should have practiced the latter, without neglecting the former. You blind guides! You strain out a gnat but swallow a camel (Matt. 23:23,24).

In their proud pursuit of the externals, the Pharisees forgot their hearts and attitudes. Those who strive for human perfection have the wrong perspective.

Maybe as you read this you find yourself struggling with arrogance and are tempted to dismiss this message because of some technical error. Dear reader, do not fall into the web of human perfectionism. It is prideful, destructive, and it causes you to strain out the gnat (the details) but swallow the camel (overlook the condition of your heart and your indifference to sin).

On a recent international trip, I arrived at a church in a poor part of town where I was to preach. As I entered the building, my eyes observed every detail in the first few seconds. As I walked down the aisle toward the front row, my soul became preoccupied with the fact that the walls did not quite reach the roof and that the floor was made out of dirt. Suddenly, something like a spiritual electric current shot through my body and I became aware of the strong presence of God in that place. All of my thoughts changed immediately. I said to myself, *Who cares about the details? God is here; this ministry time is going to be wonderful.* And it was, as hundreds repented for their sins that evening.

Have you erected a wall in your heart that is keeping you from the fire of God?

When you hear a sermon, are you one of those who thinks, *There! He made a grammatical mistake! This minister is not well trained; I wonder what his or her grade point average was? I wish I could receive this message, but the style is not up to my level.* Have you completely lost your fervor and reverence?

In Jesus' name, I urge you to resist and hate self-righteous perfectionism. It has nothing to do with purity of the heart and it offends the Lord. Take a moment right now to renounce any religious or academic arrogance. Dare to become like a child, simple and trusting. After all, that is the kind of person Jesus said would inherit the kingdom of heaven (see Matt. 18:3)! Maybe this is the barrier that has been keeping you away from the fire of God. Have you erected a fire wall in your heart? Repent now, and God will embrace you with His love!

A WORD TO MINISTERS

Dear pastor, my prayer is that your life and ministry would be transformed from the inside out by God's fire. As the Lord renewed me, the following are some of the key changes that took place in my life.

Dare to Become a Preacher of Holiness

Fellow minister, dare to risk some opposition. You may be surprised at how many people are just waiting for powerful and biblical holiness teaching and preaching. You do *not* have to become a hateful preacher with a threatening voice.

The antidote for legalism in the pulpit is to preach with tears in your eyes. Let the people know that the love of God is breaking your heart at the moment you make the altar call. Let them see that you have been crushed in His presence and now you come in humility to warn fellow Christians of the dangers of a lukewarm life.

Do Not Be Afraid to Repeat Yourself

It is okay to repeat or emphasize some subjects. You might become less original for a while, but you will also be more effective in the long run. Do not preach to impress; call them to change!

Preach Holiness with Hope

Maybe you are wondering how to have a consistent ministry of holiness without becoming a depressing, fault-finding pastor. I think the answer is to always preach holiness with hope. It is easy to do so because we are still in the day of salvation—it is not too late for forgiveness and grace for the repentant.

Make sure you allow the joy of the Lord to invade your people, especially after the most dramatic confessions of sin. After sin is gone from the heart, it leaves a spiritual vacuum. Make sure your people understand that after confession comes forgiveness from God (see 1 John 1:9). Take time to receive and enjoy His love. It is important to remain in God's presence until the Holy Spirit fills the hearts and minds with His love.

Even for the chronic penitents who come forward for every call of repentance (only to fall back into the vice), encourage them to keep seeking after God. If they have come 50 times, encourage them to come 51 times, until the bondage of sin is permanently broken and Satan gets the message. These people are bound to Christ and will begin to hate evil and resist the devil until he flees. Preach holiness with hope for everyone!

Preach Holiness with Compassion

A young lady came forward with many others. But she was not praying; she was just crying without consolation. When I went near her she said, "I don't think God can forgive me; I have had four abortions." I was deeply moved by the agony of this young lady. I then motioned to one of the ladies of our church to come and hug this girl. As she did, I told the crying lady, "Just as my sister is hugging you, so God is hugging you now!"

I believe that did it! The lady had been feeling so filthy and guilty that she could not receive my sermon on repentance and forgiveness. But by showing her compassion in a graphic way, it brought the message home. Make people feel compassion as you talk and minister to them. After all, that is what Jesus feels when we come to Him and repent.

OUR EVANGELICAL SINS

For the sinful nature desires what is contrary to the Spirit, and the Spirit what is contrary to the sinful nature. They are in conflict with each other, so that you do not do what you want.

GALATIANS 5:17

The above passage in Paul's letter to the Galatians is written to believers. This speaks about the story of Christian frustration; there are many frustrated Christians worshipping in frustrated churches with frustrated ministries. A fight is raging—a struggle between what is of the Spirit and what is of the flesh. But if you are led by the Spirit, you are not under the law. This mean you will not be at fault with the Old Testament Mosaic law, the commandment of our Lord. As we yield completely to the Holy Spirit under the New Covenant of grace, we are not under condemnation—we are free (see Rom. 8:1).

Now what follows is one of the strongest warnings to believers in the entire New Testament. These are signs of someone who has fallen into decadence, ruin and disaster: "The acts of the sinful nature are obvious: sexual immorality, impurity and debauchery" (Gal. 5:19).

You may be able to hide your adultery, even if you are a pastor. Your very own wife might not even know what has been happening in your life. But you cannot hide from God. All of our acts are clear before the presence of the Lord.

If you have committed any sexual sins (and this is especially true if you are in the ministry), I urge you to repent of immorality before putting this book down. If your eyes are not pure, you must repent this very day. First John 2:6 says, "Whoever claims to live in him must walk as Jesus did."

My brother and sister, I ask you, how did Jesus walk when He was on earth? He was 30 years old when He began His ministry, and yet He was still single. Some of you will say, "When I get married, I will be holy, but right now I cannot resist sexual temptation." But Jesus was single and was perfectly holy.

How did Jesus walk on earth? In absolute purity. If we would have stopped Him on His way out of Capernaum or any other city and said, "Jesus, can I look at Your eyes?" we would have seen the purity of heaven there. The Bible says that if we are going to remain in Him, we must walk as Jesus walked. We need the same purity.

The eyes of Jesus did not view pornographic movies or magazines, immoral women's magazines or impure literature. He was the spotless Lamb of God. And that is what He is calling us to do: to live in that kind of purity. We must grow to the stature of the fullness of Jesus Christ and nothing less (see Eph. 4:13). Tell Him, "I want to be like You, Jesus."

I pray faith comes to you so that you can believe you can be like Jesus. Some say, "How can you say that?" Jesus calls us to imitate Him, to walk like He walked:

Be perfect, therefore, as your heavenly father is perfect (Matt. 5:48).

Be imitators of God, therefore, as dearly loved children (Eph. 5:1).

Be holy, because I am holy (1 Pet. 1:16).

He overcame temptation so that we can overcome temptation. As long as we are on this side of heaven, we will be tempted. But the power of the Holy Spirit will help us walk in glory and victory. The pattern of carnality is struggle—defeat—struggle—defeat. But the pattern of the Spirit-led life is struggle—victory—struggle—victory!

TURNING FROM A DOUBLE LIFE

The acts of the sinful nature are obvious: sexual immorality, impurity and debauchery; idolatry and witchcraft; hatred, discord, jealousy, fits of rage, selfish ambition, dissensions, factions and envy; drunkenness, orgies, and the like. I warn you, as I did before, that those who live like this will not inherit the kingdom of God (Gal. 5:19-21).

Galatians 5:19-21 continues talking about the things that are contrary to the Spirit and mentions sexual immorality and impurity. Some of you may be saying, "Pastor, I have never fallen into adultery; I am a good Christian." If your thoughts are impure, however, or you hate your wife, you are living outside God's will. Or if you wish you had married someone else and if your thoughts and affections are already with someone else, you are outside the will of God. External conformity to Christian conduct will not justify inner purity. God loves you and wants to change you!

You cannot continue to live a double life. If you turn to the Lord, He will embrace you and give you the power to change your thoughts. Some people live with regrets, thinking, *I wish I would have married so-and-so. I wish I would have grown up in another city. I wish, I wish, I wish.* When the fire of the Holy Spirit comes upon you, your soul will become satisfied right where you are! There will be no impurity of any kind, nor will you live in regret.

Some Christians may be thinking, *These are just my thoughts; they do not bother anyone else. These thoughts are not causing evil.* But when we have individual sin in our lives, there is a collective effect, a Body effect. Our impure thought life does affect those around us—most directly, our spouse and children. The Lord wants to purify us and make us 100% pure.

A brother from a Christian newspaper in Argentina called me and said, "Sergio, we are very happy with what you have received from the Lord, but we have a problem. We hear that you are out there preaching that 98% holiness is not enough."

I was thinking to myself, *What is wrong with that?* I explained to him that God's Word contains many scriptures about purity. I mentioned 1 Thessalonians 5:23: "May your whole spirit, soul and body be kept blameless at the coming of our Lord Jesus Christ." I read many other scriptures as well. Finally he said, "Please come and minister to our entire staff."

No one can argue with holiness. If they are in Christ, they will believe you. Galatians 5:19 continues:

"impurity and debauchery; idolatry and witchcraft"
"Idolatry" is defined as something we admire excessively. Do you have an excessive admiration for someone or something that is taking the main place in your heart? That is idolatry!

Please pay attention to this list. So many times in the past I had skipped this list because I thought, *This is not for me because it is talking about witchcraft and idolatry.* But watch what follows in the same list:

"hatred, discord, jealousy"

If you are a person who delights in creating discord and division in your neighborhood, job or church, you are not in God's will. Do you enjoy creating and fanning the flames of resentment between one family member and another? If so, you are outside the will of God. When things go better for someone else at work or in your church and you get a sick feeling instead of rejoicing for them, this is a sign that something is not right. I plead with you: Take a few moments to repent before putting down this book.

"fits of rage"

Some men are so nice in church, but when they get home they are violent. Some verbally abuse their wives. Perhaps they think it is a sign of their masculinity, but actually they simply cannot control their mouths. They may break things at home or even hurt one of their beloved family members. I know men who have created disasters in their homes and then later cried because they wanted to change. They could not change, however, because there was a place of rebellion in their character. If your character is uncontrollable, Jesus Christ can control it. Jesus can break our character when we bring it into His presence. The Lord wants to heal those in the Church who struggle with anger and rage.

"selfish ambition"

Selfishness and misguided ambition are plagues that affect many Christians and ministries. If you come before the Lord today to repent, you must come to die to your ministry. This is not a party; this is a funeral. The Christian life begins with death, and then it moves on to resurrection in Christ.

I remember speaking to a certain city mayor who is now a dear friend of mine, and I asked him if he would like to receive Christ. He asked me, "What does that mean?"

I said, "It means what it says in Matthew 16:24: 'If anyone would come after me, he must deny himself and take up his cross and follow me.'" I added, "You will need to die to yourself and live for Jesus Christ."

He gave his life to Christ right then and there and he continues to grow in the Light. The Christian life and Christian growth begin with death. We have to die to our flesh, our sins, our evil passions, our selfishness, our aspirations—we must become totally dead to ourselves.

"dissensions, and factions"

These are also things the Lord hates.

"and envy, drunkenness, orgies and the like"

As I was ministering in a conference full of Christian leaders and pastors, I had them hold the hand of the person next to them and pray this unselfish prayer: "Lord, bless my brother more than me. May his church grow larger than mine. Cause the other local congregations to grow so much that my church of 2,000 will be the smallest."

If you get sick with envy when you hear about the success of another pastor in your city, you need to repent.

A STRONG WARNING IN THE NEW TESTAMENT

Now come some of the strongest words in the New Testament. In Galatians 5:21 Paul says, "I warn you, as I did before, that those who live like this will not inherit the kingdom of God."

My friends, that is a repeated warning in the Scriptures. Some people think, *Grace—the grace of the Lord will cleanse me next Sunday.* On Monday this person returns to his vice, to his X-rated movies or to whatever is polluting his spiritual life. On the great judgment day, there will be people who will come confidently into the presence of Jesus and say, "Lord Jesus, we had a ministry of deliverance in our church."

He will demand of them, "Why do you call Me Lord? I don't know you. You have not obeyed My will. You have done your own thing and you have used My gifts for your own glory!" (see Matt. 7:21-23).

Others will come to Him and say, "Lord Jesus, we had a ministry of healing in our church. In Your name we healed the sick."

And the Lord will tell them, "I don't know you; you disobeyed Me!" He may even say, "I told you time and again, through My servants and My Word, that those who practice such things will not inherit the kingdom of God. You did not believe Me or take My Word seriously."

Someone may say, "But Lord, I had only one small habit of lying. The rest of my Christian life was good." And the Lord is going to tell this individual, "Didn't I tell you that liars would not enter into the kingdom of heaven?"

Those who do not obey will not enter the Kingdom, even though they have the gifts of the Holy Spirit working in their lives. Those who harden their hearts and live a unrepentant lifestyle of sin will not make it. They are willfully resisting the Holy Spirit, even if their sins are not spectacular.

NO BRIBERY IN HEAVEN

In my country, bribery was once a widespread problem. It was not uncommon to be pulled over by a policeman and be cited for some random infraction of the law, even if you had done nothing wrong. But all it took was a little cash and you would be happily on your way—that is why you were stopped in the first place. This habit corrupted an entire nation.

If you are not walking in the will of God, you need to wake up now!

But there will be no bribery in heaven. You will not be able to say, "Jesus, wait a moment before You throw me out and toss me into hell. I know pastor so-and-so who is already here. I have references and good contacts in the evangelical world." Listen to me: Your church title will not matter much on that day. If you are not walking in alignment with the will of God, you need to wake up now!

Those who have not taken seriously the commandments of the Lord are going to go through something like what happened in the days of Noah. Noah told the people, "Rain is coming; a flood is coming." They made fun of him and his message; they did not believe it was true. Noah and his family entered into the ark and God shut the door (see Gen. 7). Once the door is closed, there will be no possibility of it opening again.

The Lord has sent me to preach a message of warning.

Why don't you take a moment right now to look through this list again, and let the Holy Spirit point out areas of sin of which you need to repent. Do it now.

These are the acts of the sinful nature as described in Galatians 5:19-21:

- *Sexual immorality*—adultery, fornication and/or immoral fantasies
- *Impurity*—something offensive or contaminating; pornography
- *Debauchery*—gross indulgence in one's sensual appetites
- *Idolatry*—excessive admiration
- *Witchcraft*—practices or powers of witches or wizards
- *Hatred*—intense dislike or aversion to another
- *Discord*—lack of agreement; conflict; strife
- *Jealousy*—attitude, feeling or condition of being displaced by a rival
- *Fits of rage*—violent anger, wrath or fury
- *Selfish ambition*—eager desire for one's own success
- *Dissensions*—differences of opinion arising from anger
- *Factions*—a group of people operating within and often in opposition to another group
- *Envy*—a feeling of resentment or discontent over another's superior attainments
- *Drunkenness*—result of drinking alcoholic beverages to excess
- *Orgies*—any excessive indulgence[1]

REMOVE THE SPLINTERS

When I was a child, my mom instructed us that we could not run in the house, especially not barefoot. The reason was that the wooden floor in our home produced many splinters. But we were not always obedient.

One day, Mom was not home and my sister and I were running full speed through the house. Sure enough, a sliver lodged very deep in my foot. I was very young and I was very scared. I decided that when my mom came back, I would not show her my problem. I would just try to act like nothing was wrong. Every hour that went by, the splinter hurt more, but I was forced to continue acting like nothing was wrong.

I had decided that I would rather live with that splinter than face the punishment of my mother. Plus, I knew that my mother would be very "cruel" if I let her know I had a problem with my foot. She would take the tweezers and mercilessly make me suffer for *one second* while she pulled the splinter out! I did not want to suffer even for that one second. Instead, I suffered for four days, all the while trying to act like nothing was wrong.

Some Christians live their lives this way. They say, "I am okay, Lord. Everything is fine. Just a little evil here and there, but nothing major." Yet all along they are limping as they walk. Some people in the kingdom of God say, "Lord, I am 95% holy. It is only one sliver, one small infection. I can live with it." But the Holy Spirit wants to get your attention, grab you with His love and tear out the sin in your life.

Many Christian men walk with a limp for years, even men in the ministry. They say to themselves, *I am a servant of God, but I have a small problem with pornography*. Do you know what God wants to do with pornography? He wants to take His tweezers and pull it out of your eyes and soul forever so that your eyes will shine with the purity of Jesus.

After a few days of walking around with the splinter in my foot, it began to get infected. Finally, my mother detected something was very wrong. She said, "Child, come here." She sat me on a chair, picked up my foot and, without any anesthesia, took out that splinter. Within a few hours, I felt a difference and was able to walk better.

Likewise, the Lord is nearby and even more anxious to remove splinters from the heart. Many of you have been carrying splinters that you do not have to carry. Some of you may say, "Oh, it is because of my character. You know, Sergio, it is because I am a depressed person. My grandfather was depressed, my aunt was depressed, my next door neighbor is depressed, so I should be depressed." You walk with a limp because you have the splinter of depression in your heart. Give your depression to the Lord.

DEPRESSION IS NOT PART OF THE PACKAGE OF THE GOSPEL

I remember my years of depression. That was my wilderness. I was in the ministry, teaching and preaching God's Word. I would finish my sermon and I would see some results, but I could hardly wait to get to my room to be alone. Sometimes I would cry and I did not know why. I was a melancholic. Those of you who have gone through this know what I am talking about. But do you know what the problem was? I thought depression was part of the package.

I accepted depression as my companion until the Lord began to give me authority. And in the dorm room of my university I put up a sign saying, "In the name of Jesus, I reject depression from my life." My friends would come to my room and say, "Wow, that is a strong statement." I was a little bit embarrassed that they would read the sign. Basically, I wanted the demons to read it!

Brother and sister, I want to encourage your faith and tell you today that the Lord has healed me completely from depression. He gave me a ministry to those who are depressed, including ministers that suffer in its grip.

I have heard people say, "Brother, depression is not a sin, it is just a sickness." Well then, pray for healing. The problem comes when we say, "Depression, since I cannot overcome you, you and I will become good friends. I do not drink alcohol, but you will be my vice. We will be together the rest of my life." Do not welcome depression into your life. Do not welcome self-pity and melancholy. The Lord wants to heal you so He can use you.

Note

1. Most of these definitions and additional notes were taken from *Funk & Wagnall's Standard Dictionary* (New York, NY: HarperCollins Publishers, Inc., 1993).

SELF-EXAMINATION AND THE CALL TO REPENTANCE

The medical community uses the powerful tool of mass education to help us detect certain diseases in their early stages. Doctors first educate us about the various risks and signs of disease, such as cancer, and then teach us techniques for self-examination. This process saves many lives by putting tools into the hands of common people. The result is that we are often able to recognize symptoms and detect diseases in time to do something about them.

These methods for disease detection are called diagnostic tools. That is what I would like to do now in the spiritual realm: conduct a diagnostic examination of our hearts and minds. Please take a few moments to examine your own life. This is a call to Christians who live in sin. If you are doing well and the holiness of God has taken over your life, rejoice. But this prayer is for brothers and sisters who are entangled in sin. You may be a sincere person who wants revival and prays for the glory of the Lord to come to your city. But before God can take your city, He wants to take your heart.

COME AS YOU ARE

Let the Holy Spirit do His work in your heart right now. Some of you have been distracted by many things, but the Lord wants just one thing from you. If you dare to give him 100% of your life unconditionally, from that moment on the Lord will take over. He is not saying, "Change your habits and then come to Me." He is saying, "Just as you are, please come." He is a God of mercy. The old hymn we used to sing for the unconverted can be sung today for every Christian bound by sin:

> Just as I am without one plea, but that Thy blood was shed for me. And that Thou biddest me come to Thee, O Lamb of God, I come, I come. ("Just As I Am," Charlotte Elliott, 1836)

Some people say, "Pastor, I want to believe this, but I do not know if I can." First Corinthians 1:30 tells us that "Jesus Christ . . . has become for us wisdom from God—that is, our righteousness, holiness and redemption." Purity is by faith. We become pure when we embrace the feet of Jesus Christ and He imparts His holiness to us. Purity is not self-discipline (although it includes self-discipline) but a miracle from heaven. We are changed when the eyes of Jesus look into our eyes and hearts and He begins to remove all the sin that remains. Jesus will impart more and more of His purity to you as you receive more and more of Him!

Some of you have repented for years for your sin and you say, "How can I repent again for the same sin? I would rather go on sinning than to repent and sin again." Please do not give up hope, my brother and sister. The Lord will not only forgive you, but will also give you power over sin. I pray that a righteous and anointed anger against sin would come into your life right now.

Father, I pray for those who have been making covenant with sin and with the enemy, that they would reject the sin from their lives. Some of you may be saying, "I wish I could get God's permission to commit adultery." You are entangled in your emotions and affections. Some of you might say, "I am resisting sin, but my heart is somewhere else." Right now, I pray that the Lord would give you a righteous anger against sin! The Bible tells us in Psalm 119:128:

And because I consider all your precepts right, I hate every wrong path.

This is the Word of the Lord for you!

NOT ASHAMED TO REPENT

For those of you who may be in sin, forget about everything else right now. The time is coming when you will give an account of yourself before God (see Rom. 14:10-12). When Jesus Christ died on the cross, He did not do it privately. He was not embarrassed to confess us before the Father. Why should we be scared, ashamed or embarrassed to repent before God Almighty? Let the Lord speak to your heart right now and point out areas He wants to change. Even as you take a few moments now to examine yourself, remember that the Lord Jesus walked a long road to Mount Calvary. He died for you and me in the very prime of His life at the young age of 33.

Several months after I received this precious fire of the Holy Spirit, I went back to visit the Brownsville Revival and rejoiced as many people came forward to repent and renew their lives. I was sitting in the pew when the Holy Spirit told me, "You go, too." I said, "But Lord, I just gave my testimony to my friends sitting with me of how You empowered me and now they will see me repenting. I will look like a hypocrite."

But I obeyed the Holy Spirit and went forward. As I knelt down, the Holy Spirit said, "You have one idol left." The Lord spoke to me and said, "Your love for your children is so strong that you are ready to put Me in second place." I knelt down and repented for the sin of idolatry and I received forgiveness.

TAKE ACTION NOW

Take a moment right now to kneel down and begin to tell your Lord what is wrong with your life. You will no longer have to live your Christian life with a limp. Allow Him to take the splinter out of your heart. Just as it says in Zechariah 3:9, in a single day the Lord can remove the sin of His people. The Lord is present, and He can impart His holiness upon your life.

It is okay to cry for your sin. Let the Lord break your heart over your sin. Let the Holy Spirit reveal to you the seriousness of your transgression. Just taking the effort to kneel down, for some, is a step of faith. We must believe in the promises of the Lord. Jesus is the baptizer. He will give us the baptism of the Holy Spirit and fire. He will impart His holiness upon us, but we must repent and confess. There is no revival without repentance and the purging of the Church. Come to Jesus; He loves you. If you can physically, kneel down right where you are and begin to pray.

Those who feel filthy and dirty might ask, "How can the Lord even deal with me?" The Lord specializes in people like you. He loves you. All of us have fallen short of the glory of God (see Rom. 3:23). The Lord died for that reason, so that you do not have to die for your sin. Just come to Him and receive Him.

The only thing that can stop you from coming to Jesus with your sin now is either shame or pride. Set that aside and come. The Lord is inviting every person who is not sure of his or her purity and salvation to come to Him. If you are saying, "I am not sure if all of my sins are forgiven," come to Jesus. If you are doubting, doubt your doubts and believe your faith. Come to Him with your burdens and your sadness. Come even with church problems that have burdened you in the past. Leave them at His feet.

Allow the Lord to set you free today!

You may be saying, "Pastor, I have been repenting for this same sin for 25 years." I say to you, come and repent once more! "Taste and see that the Lord is good" (Ps. 34:8). If you are hooked on pornography, drugs or alcohol, come to Jesus. If you are hooked on hatred, criticism or division, come and the Lord will set you free.

One brother came to me from Europe and said, "Pastor, I have a lovely wife and three wonderful children, but my marriage is being destroyed because I am hooked on pornography."

Immediately I sensed the compassion of God descending upon me. All I did was give him a hug and I said, "The Lord has done it already." In his confession, he was set free. The power of God set him free. Confess your areas of need to the Lord and allow Him to set you free today!

CALL IT WHAT IT IS

Once you have repented for your own sin, you may want to repent for your city or your nation. The following prayer was prayed at a National Day of Prayer event in Ft. Worth, Texas:

> *Lord, forgive us for being politically correct instead of biblically and morally correct.*
>
> *Lord, forgive us for violence in our homes, in our streets and in our schools.*
>
> *Lord, have mercy on us and forgive us for racism, sexism and intolerance.*
>
> *Father, forgive us for the abortions, pornography, and child molestations.*
>
> *Purify your people, Lord. Purify the Church, and then purify this nation.*
>
> *Forgive us for calling it an alternative lifestyle instead of an immoral lifestyle.*
>
> *Forgive us for calling it safe sex instead of illicit sex.*
>
> *Forgive those who preach justification for everybody, instead of justification for the repentant.*
>
> *Forgive us for our fear of responsibility and accountability, while insisting upon our rights.*
>
> *Forgive us, Lord, for polluting the environment, not only physically, but also morally.*
>
> *Have mercy, Lord.*

PSALM 51 PRAYER

We do not need to hide our sins. We can confess them, for "He is faithful and just and will forgive us our sins and purify us from all unrighteousness" (1 John 1:9). Please pray the following prayer with all the strength of your heart. You must pray with faith and believe that today you are entering into new ground.

Rest is available for the people of God; today you can enter into that rest. As the Lord receives this prayer of repentance, He will turn your mourning into joy. As some of you pray this prayer, there will even be sickness that will leave. As the Lord heals the heart of the Church, many of you will be healed physically. Pray this prayer (adapted from Psalm 51) right now; it will be heard in heaven and will echo in hell:

Father God, I recognize that I need You. I have sinned and I ask Your forgiveness.

I realize that Jesus paid the price on the cross of Calvary, so Lord, forgive me of all my sins.

Lord, I ask You to change my life today.

From this day on, I want to walk like Jesus walked.

I want to be like Jesus; I want to have the mind of Christ.

I want to walk in the power of the Holy Spirit.

Have mercy on me, O God, according to Your unfailing love; according to Your great compassion, blot out my transgressions.

Wash away all of my iniquity and cleanse me from my sin,

For I know my transgressions and my sin is always before me.

Against You, You only, have I sinned and done what is evil in Your sight.

Surely You desire truth in the inner parts; You teach me wisdom in the inmost place.

Cleanse me with hyssop, and I will be clean; wash me, and I will be whiter than snow.

Let me hear joy and gladness; let the bones You have crushed rejoice.

Hide Your face from my sins and blot out all my iniquity.

Create in me a pure heart, O God, and renew a steadfast spirit within me.

Do not cast me from Your presence or take Your Holy Spirit from me.

Restore to me the joy of Your salvation and grant me a willing spirit, to sustain me.

Amen!

Now say to Him:

Thank You, Lord, for loving me so much.
Thank You for Your forgiveness;
I receive Your forgiveness.
I cannot pay You in any way for Your forgiveness.
Thank You for Jesus who paid the price.
Now I receive Your forgiveness, Lord.
And now I receive the purity of Jesus Christ in my life.

If you could just understand how much the Lord loves you. Jesus is walking into the room right now to hug you, just like the father hugged the prodigal son (see Luke 15:20). You will no longer be tormented by your failures. Even in your failures you will glorify Jesus Christ, and God will bring victory to your life.

If you want the baptism of the Holy Spirit and fire, the Lord has already said yes to you! Do you want it? He will give it to you. We humans are not that good, and yet if our children ask us for bread, we do not throw a stone on their heads. We love them and we give them what they need. And yet how much more will our heavenly Father give the Holy Spirit and fire to those who ask for it. Some of you need a baptism of faith to believe this is possible. Just pray what the father of the demon-possessed boy said in Mark 9:24: "I do believe; help me overcome my unbelief!"

THE THREE PS OF THE FIRE: PURITY, POWER AND PASSION

Before the fire of God came into my life, I also struggled against sin, and the battles were lengthy. When the fire of holiness came upon me, I noticed that the battles became shorter. The fire of purity will come and give you authority against sin. The fire of the Holy Spirit brings three things: purity, power against sin and Satan, and passion for God and for the lost.

I had always been a person who witnessed to lost people about God's salvation. But after the fire came over my life, I began to witness like never before. How many of you travel on airplanes? You have a wonderful evangelistic field there, because people cannot get off of an airplane! You can preach to them and they will listen.

After receiving this baptism of fire, the first person I witnessed to was a 19-year-old man on an airplane. You see, I know the Four Spiritual Laws and other wonderful Christian witnessing tools. But as I looked at this young man and opened my mouth, the Holy Spirit took over. I said, "Do you know what the Lord has done for me? For six days I was shaking under the presence of Almighty God!" I got his attention!

I could see tears in his eyes right away; I did not understand why. I said to myself, *This is the worst evangelistic method I have ever used!* Sometimes the Holy Spirit says, "Preacher, step aside.

I want to talk to that person!" That young man was deeply touched by the message of the gospel. Another young man I talked to on a plane accepted Christ right away.

Let the power of God use you! Let the Holy Spirit take over your life. We read in Acts 1:8 the words of Jesus to the apostles:

> You will receive power when the Holy Spirit comes upon you; and you will be my witnesses in [your city] and in [your state] and [your country] and to the ends of the earth.

In reality, this baptism of the Holy Spirit is not an option; it is vital. The Bible says to "be filled with the Spirit" (Eph. 5:18). Being indwelled with the Spirit and being filled with the Spirit are two different things. It is the difference between music playing in one room of a house or having the entire house filled with music to the point that the neighbors and passersby can hear it. You can have a light on in your bedroom, or you can light the entire house inside and out until your property is flooded with light. You can have a guest staying in the guest room of your home, or you can welcome the guest and allow him to occupy the entire house. Likewise, you can "have the Spirit" or you can "be filled with the Spirit."

Some people worry about the right timing for the fire to fall on their lives. I can tell you that in my own life it came at the "wrong" moment. I was not ready for it. I had so many things to do. I pray that the Lord will disrupt your sense of timing, interrupt your agenda and kidnap you!

8

FALSE CONVERSIONS
AND GOD'S FIRE

On a recent trip to New York, I was riding in a taxi and began to speak to John, the 21-year-old driver, about Christ. He told me he had left his home because his mother used drugs and he wanted to find a better life. I asked him, "John, have you been born again?"

"Yes," he said.

"Are you sure that you are saved?" I countered.

Again his answer was, "Yes, I attend a [certain denomination] church."

I talked with him a while longer and asked him about other aspects of his life and he told me, "I am living with a girl. She is not my wife, but we want to have a baby."

That gave me another entry point with him. I said, "John, the way of the Lord is not like that. The way of the Lord is a road of obedience to the Word of God." I began to explain the gospel to him and he began to understand. I told him, "Sex is only for married couples, but you are living with this girl without being committed to her in marriage. You are hoping to have a baby, but how is God going to bless this baby if you do not receive His blessing by being married?"

ASSURANCE OF HEAVEN?

I realized that this young man, John, was convinced he was saved, but he did not understand anything about the gospel. Not only that, but he also had other addictions and bondages in his life.

At first I was impacted by the security with which this young man had responded to me. I was intimidated and I wavered on whether or not to announce the good news to him. Second, I was taken aback by the evidence that he did not really know the Lord Jesus Christ. Thankfully, I was able to share the Word of the Lord with him.

Our world is filled with people who say, "Don't talk to me about Christ; I already have religion." But my concern is *not* whether you have religion, but whether or not you have Jesus Christ. Have you been born again? You may say, "Oh yes, I have been an evangelical Christian for 20 years." So what does that mean? Do you know how many evangelicals are going to hell? I believe there will be an entire neighborhood of evangelicals in hell, people who believed themselves to be something they were not.[1]

For many of you, I know this message does not bring much peace. But I would ask you to just allow the Holy Spirit, through His Word, to take hold of the scalpel. In the hands of the Master, the scalpel is not a dagger but a remedy that removes all spiritual infection and then heals us completely.

God knows everything about you—about all of us. He knows all about John's life, and I know that the Holy Spirit is working in him. Because God opened a door for John, he understood that beyond the religiosity, he needed to repent and to return to the commandments of the Lord.

But how about you, reader? How is your life today? Do you know that two centuries ago, Charles Finney preached on this same topic of false conversion? I discovered that Finney also confronted the issue of people who think they are going to heaven and who think they are of God. But as it was in Finney's time, there are those in today's Church who are not headed for heaven. Rather, they have been given a false hope.

GRACE DOES NOT COVER UNCONFESSED SIN

A pastor from Baltimore, Bart Pierce, gave me a book by Charles Finney called *Power from on High* (Whitaker House, 1996). On page 70, Finney writes, "It was not by accident that the law preceded grace." What this means is that the law of God, His commandments, prepared the way for the gospel. If one avoids looking at the law, he avoids being instructed in his soul and wants to receive the gospel of grace directly. Without repentance, however, a person creates a false hope, a false standard of the Christian experience. As it says in James 2:17, "Faith by itself, if it is not accompanied by action, is dead." If we embrace grace but never give our will and our lives over to God, practicing licentiousness and a carnal lifestyle, then have we truly entered into conversion? This faulty belief system is filling churches with false conversions.

Minister of the gospel, we must lead people to Christ by teaching them that they need a Savior, not just a blessing.

In Argentina, more than 90% of the population professes to be Christian of one denomination or another, with the majority professing to be Catholic. However, we are not seeing a country functioning according to the commandments of the Lord. The same people who swear by the Bible are the same ones who, many times, contradict that Word upon which they swore.

This mystery is explained by Jesus when He shares the Parable of the Weeds (see Matt. 13:24-30,36-43). We know that God is not dividing the wheat from the weeds right now; the Bible says that the wheat and the weeds—the truly converted and those who look like they are converted—will grow together. I am talking about those who are Christians and those who look like Christians but are not. The judgment of God has not yet fallen. "The sons of the evil one" (v. 38) and those who are falsely converted will be divided out and separated from the righteous on the day of the Lord.

This message can be a little difficult to receive for some, but it is critical. God wants us to be uncomfortable now, rather than uncomfortable on the day of the final judgment. It is better to have a little discomfort now when God stirs our souls and calls us to repentance. Incomparably worse would be to suffer the discomfort of being sent to hell on the Day of the Lord.

God is just and His laws will not be mocked (see Gal. 6:7). For the gospel to be the gospel, there has to be a message of repentance. There has to be a change of attitude and a change of conduct. Before Christ preached in the world, John the Baptist came first and prepared the way of the Lord. He said, "Repent, for the kingdom of heaven is near" (Matt. 3:2). In the same way, the Lord speaks to us today, not only with love, but also with severity (see Matt. 4:17).

TRUE VERSUS FALSE CONVERSIONS

What does "conversion" mean? It means to completely change direction. Before conversion, we were headed in our own direction, doing whatever we thought best. We governed our own lives, whether God liked it or not. But when a person becomes converted, he or she changes direction, moves to a new address (spiritually speaking) and returns to Jesus Christ. It is not only a change of heart. It is not only a change of emotions. It is a change in behavior—in the way we manage finances, speak with our neighbors, treat our employees and so on. It is a total change; it is radical and strong.

Let us look at Matthew 25:1-13, the Parable of the Ten Virgins. This parable will help each one of us to know whether we are truly converted or if we have experienced a false conversion. This Word is for everyone:

> At that time the kingdom of heaven will be like ten virgins who took their lamps and went out to meet the bridegroom. Five of them were foolish and five were wise. The foolish ones took their lamps but did not take any oil with them. The wise, however, took oil in jars along with their lamps. The bridegroom was a long time in coming, and they all became drowsy and fell asleep. At midnight the cry rang out: "Here's the bridegroom! Come out to meet him!"
>
> Then all the virgins woke up and trimmed their lamps. The foolish ones said to the wise, "Give us some of your oil; our lamps are going out."
>
> "No," they replied, "there may not be enough for both us and you. Instead, go to those who sell oil and buy some for yourselves."
>
> But while they were on their way to buy the oil, the bridegroom arrived. The virgins who were ready went in with him to the wedding banquet. And the door was shut.
>
> Later the others also came. "Sir! Sir!" they said. "Open the door for us!"

But he replied, "I tell you the truth, I don't know you." Therefore keep watch, because you do not know the day or the hour.

These ten virgins represent the Church of Jesus Christ. They were already invited to the wedding feast; their names were already on the list. They were people who knew the things of God. Today the Bridegroom, Jesus Christ, is hoping we are in the bridal party. But *not all of us* are ready. Not all of us have turned from a faithless, carnal life.

The Bible also speaks to us about the last days. My friends, we need to pray, because the coming days may be very difficult. We the Church, being the Bride, should be watching and praying. We cannot doze off into a spiritual sleep while we are on planet Earth. We need to wake up—and stay awake! As the verse says, "Wake up, O sleeper, rise from the dead, and Christ will shine on you" (Eph. 5:14).

Romans 14:10,11 says that we will all stand before God's judgment seat and that every knee will bow before the Lord; every tongue will confess to God. Notice that it does not say all the knees of the evangelicals will bow or all the knees of the Catholics or all those that went to church. Rather, it says that *every* knee is going to bow. When God resurrects Mr. Adolf Hitler from the dead to give an account of what he did while on earth, he will have to bow before almighty God and say, "You are the Lord!"

The whole human race will bow and give honor to the King of kings and Lord of lords. He lives forever! He has all power in heaven and in earth. But for a time, the Lord gives permission to the devil to lead those astray who want to follow another road. Those who want to go to hell can go freely. Nobody will be in heaven because they were forced to go. Those that get to heaven will be there because they repented and loved the things of God.

Today you may not be sure whether you will go to heaven or hell—if you will go upward or downward. I tell you in the name of Jesus: There is salvation in Christ. God will embrace you, forgive your sins and give you strength to live in purity for the rest of your days.

My brother and sister, the lamps spoken of in the Parable of the Ten Virgins represent our hearts. I ask you, is your heart on fire? Is your lamp prepared?

Not long ago I arrived in Baltimore to minister at Rock City Church. In the afternoon before I was to speak, I knelt down in my hotel room and said to the Lord, "I am more concerned about my fatigue than for lost souls. Forgive me and give me a passion for souls. Please give me tears, once again, for the lost. Let me feel the pain—the feeling that Jesus had for those who were sick and tormented when He walked on this earth." And the Lord did it. Then in New York, the place I visited after Baltimore, it came even stronger; it broke my heart.

APATHY OR COMPASSION?

Do you want the compassion of God to break your apathy and fill your heart with fire? By the grace of God, since Kathy and I received the fire, we have ministered to thousands of people in Asia, Europe, the United States and Latin America. Do you know what the most repeated prayer request is? "Pastor, please pray for me so that I will receive your passion for lost souls."

How is your heart, reader? How is your spiritual temperature? Are you on medium, low or is only the pilot light on? The Bible speaks of lamps. The ten virgins, representing the Church, all had oil lamps. But five of the virgins were foolish; they were careless and senseless. The senseless ones took the lamps of religiosity.

They apparently did what they were supposed to do, but they did not have the anointing. The oil of the Spirit in their lives was low and their lamps were doomed not to last very long. Religion, without the power of God, does not last very long.

Is your heart's fire set on medium? Low?
Or is only the pilot light on?

Brother and sister, take care not to embrace religion without the manifestation of the Holy Spirit. Young person, make sure that your life is saturated with the presence of God. If the oil of the Holy Spirit does not descend into your heart, you are in danger! Days of great fervor have to come to the Church, a fervor stronger than ever before.

A man who had been in our church more than 20 years came to me and said, "Pastor, today I have decided that I am going to give all of my life to Jesus Christ." I pray it will not take you so long to come to that decision. I pray that if you have not given all of your life to the Lord, or if the flame in your heart has gone out, today you would receive the oil of the Holy Spirit.

The wise, however, took oil in jars along with their lamps. The bridegroom was a long time in coming and they all became drowsy and fell asleep (Matt. 25:4,5).

What happened to the bridegroom? He was "a long time in coming." Some think, *So much time has gone by and Jesus still does not come. I will take advantage of the time and live my life as I please.*

They all became drowsy and fell asleep. At midnight the cry rang out (Matt. 25:5,6).

Perhaps tonight at midnight a cry will go out, the trumpets will sound and a strong voice from heaven will say, "Here comes the King of kings and Lord of lords!" (1 Thess. 4:16,17). Will you be ready? Will you go with the bridegroom or will you be left behind?

Here's the bridegroom! Come out to meet him! (Matt. 25:6).

Those that did not have enough oil missed him because they had gone to look for more oil. They arrived too late! How many know that there is a time that is called "too late"? There is time in the past, time in the present, time in the future and lost time. Lost time is gone; it is over. A moment will arrive when this prophecy will no longer apply: "Now is the day of salvation" (2 Cor. 6:2). No more sermons will be preached. The Holy Spirit is calling today for the Church to be fervent in her faith.

Some may say, "But pastor, I am already converted, thank you." Brother and sister, are you really converted? How can you know? Here are several signs of people who believe they are converted but in fact are not.

SIGNS OF THE FALSELY CONVERTED

The evangelist Charles Finney mentions some of the following points in his book *Power from on High*. Because you may struggle with one or more of these signs does not mean you definitely are not converted. Only the Lord knows your heart. We all struggle with one or more of these signs at one time or another. However, if you have given yourself over to a lifestyle that is permeated with these signs, you need to seriously seek the Lord.

Resistance to Conviction

The person that is falsely converted resists all conviction of sin. Some people take out a shield during the church service and try to defend themselves during the sermon. Do not defend yourself anymore; if it is of God, receive it!

Without Repentance

The falsely converted refuse to admit their sins to the people against whom they have sinned. They might have stolen from someone but will say to themselves, *I will ask forgiveness of God at the altar*. On Monday they do not go to the person and say, "Here is the $150 that I took off your desk when you were away at lunch." They believe they have made amends because they went to the altar, but there is no fruit of repentance. Their conversion is false.

I hope that when we are in heaven, no one in hell will be able to point their finger at me and say, "Pastor, why didn't you tell me? Why didn't you warn me that if I did these things, I was not going to get into the kingdom of heaven! Why weren't you more clear in your preaching?" Thankfully, many preachers today choose to be very clear, risking status, image and the possibility that someone might be offended by their preaching. I beg you not to be offended, because the one who is writing these words is a sinner who has repented and been pardoned by the grace of Jesus. If not, I would be going to the very same hell with many others. My life would be a disaster, like that of those who do not have Christ.

I do not come to you with pride. I come to you with a restless heart, because God is speaking very clearly in these days. He loves you, and for that reason He is calling you to possess the oil of the Holy Spirit and to produce the fruit of repentance.

Broken Relationships

Falsely converted people refuse to restore relationships or make restitution toward their enemies or with people whom they have offended.

Not Watching or Waiting

The falsely converted person is not watching and waiting as the Word of God tells us to do (see Matt. 25:13). Rather, he or she is distracted and does not care.

Some time ago I was preaching at a large meeting in New York. I noticed that a lot of people were not receiving the message. It is hard when you are preaching and you realize that the people are not receiving. Finally, the Lord said to me, "There is a spirit of religiosity and 'church building' here." Because these people normally attended services in a church building, they thought that the building would save them. They believed that all was well with them.

That was when the preaching began to turn into a hammer. The Word of God is like a hammer and like fire (see Jer. 23:29). The Word of God does not return void (see Isa. 55:11). It hits and hits and hits until sooner or later something happens.

Because they were not receiving, I decided not to look at them anymore. I thought, *If I look at them, I will get distracted. Something is not right.* Maybe they thought that I was going to preach a message and say, "Come and receive all the blessings of God. It does not matter if you are repentant. It does not matter if you change your life or not. We have 'all you can eat' for everyone." But God had given me a different message.

When I made the altar call, only two people came forward in a stadium of thousands. I had never seen such a response in all the months I had been preaching about the fire of God. Usually, people come running to the altar to repent. I just closed my eyes and said, "Lord, do what You want." And the Lord began to tell me, "Keep insisting. I am saving souls." He assured me that He was there and that I should continue inviting people to repent.

When I opened my eyes, the altar was full and the people continued to come. God began to reveal to the people that religion does not save. A denomination does not save. Going to church—even though it is good—does not save. Only repentance and the power of the blood of Christ saves! Too many people go to the altar to "fix" what is wrong. God does not only want to repair your sins. He wants to do a complete overhaul—a transformation by His Holy Spirit.

Prayerlessness

Falsely converted people are lazy and impatient in waiting on the presence of God. They don't have time to pray. They don't have time for God because they don't love God—they love the world.

Do you know how many believers in the Church love worldliness? They have lost their first love for God! They say, "But I am converted. Twenty years ago I raised my hand and went forward." So what does that mean? Where is the oil? Where is the flame of the Holy Spirit that should be burning in their lives? What happened to the fire of God?

The depth of our prayer life will determine the depth to which God will use us. We must spend time with the Lord, praying and seeking His face. As we spend time with Him, His character, purity and passion will become imprinted upon our hearts and souls.

FILL YOUR LAMPS

A moment comes when the Christian who is falsely converted loses the fear of God. The Word does not make any impact on his life. This person can watch a Christian video, hear a wonderful message or attend a great conference, but nothing impacts him. It is because his heart has dried up. Today is the day, Church of Jesus, to look for oil in the presence of God. It is time to return to your first love. Some may say, "I am pretty good." That is not enough! You have to live in total purity. "And if I fail?" You get on your knees and ask for forgiveness! Either in purity or in repentance!

Many times while ministering in the United States, I have sung the song "Revival Fire Fall" by Paul Baloche. What a beautiful song of revival. But since the fire fell upon my life, I cannot sing it standing up. How strong it is when this fire falls upon you. That is what God wants to do in your life! But it will cost you. Evangelist Billy Graham once said, "Salvation is free, but discipleship will cost you everything you have."

You may ask, "How long will you preach the gospel this way?" Until the Lord comes. I will continue until the Church is so sanctified that each believer goes out and heals the sick in the hospitals, until the churches are filled with thousands of people, until cities are turned right side up with the gospel.

It is a privilege to serve the Church of Jesus Christ, but the Church lacks repentance. Falsehood and hypocrisy still abound; many people are still playing at Christianity. It is my duty, in Jesus' name, to give you a word of warning: A day will soon arrive when the oil, the little that you have left, will run out. You need to seek the presence of God. You need to come into His presence and make it your first priority to repent.

Therefore keep watch, because you do not know the day or the hour (Matt. 25:13).

I am coming soon. Hold on to what you have, so that no one will take your crown (Rev. 3:11).

Behold, I come like a thief! Blessed is he who stays awake and keeps his clothes with him, so that he may not go naked and be shamefully exposed (Rev. 16:15).

Do you have the oil of the Spirit flowing in your life? Are you shining? Do you love God with all your heart? If not, the Bible itself questions the genuineness of your "salvation."

Sometimes we have counseled people who ask, "Pastor, have I committed the unpardonable sin?"

I say to them, "No, because if you had committed it, you would not even be concerned about it." When you commit the unpardonable sin, blasphemy against the Holy Spirit, the Holy Spirit withdraws; there is no longer any conviction of sin. Thank God there is still hope.

If you are constantly critical, you have let the love of God grow cold in your life. It does not matter how long you have been a believer; you need to repent. A new believer once asked me, "Could it be that a human being can be physically alive but spiritually dead?" I was so happy to hear the question because I realized that he was beginning to understand how things really are in the spiritual realm.

When the father saw his prodigal son arrive, the son was dirty, smelling of a pigpen. But the father did not say, "Give him a bath first!" Rather, he threw his arms around his son's neck and kissed him (see Luke 15:20). Are you a prodigal? Many Christians have taken a leave from the ways of the Lord. Do not try to fix everything and then come to Jesus. Come as you are. Repentance is the first step.

Brothers and sisters, the Spirit of the Lord has hidden His face from those with a religious spirit. Some of you reading this book have grown cold in your heart and do not sense the presence of the Lord in your life. If that describes you, take a moment right now and repent for the coldness of your soul.

Others who are reading this are proud and self-righteous. Maybe you have never really known the power of the gospel. You do not behave like a Christian, nor do you fear God. Perhaps you are the most difficult to save. You know a lot of facts about Christianity and may say, "I have a position in the church. I have attended church for 25 years." If your lamp is going out, what does it matter how long you have been hanging around the church?

What are you waiting for to repent? For angels to come and get you? They will not, because the Lord respects your decision to seek Him or not. Every lukewarm Christian needs to take a moment right now and turn his or her face, again, toward God. He could be saving the best wine for last. Your relationship with Him may be better than ever before in your life. Do not delay; do it today.

Note

1. I know there will be some who will want me to answer specifically the question, How much sin disqualifies us from heaven? I would have to reply in this way: Any unconfessed sin, big or small, that one is aware of and refuses to change or repent of, has the potential to contaminate his or her whole life. "Don't you know that a little yeast works through the whole batch of dough?" (1 Cor. 5:6). It could be the symptom of a preexisting inward state of rebellion against God. It is not the amount of sin that tips the scale but, rather, the attitude toward that sin and toward Christ.

WARNING SIGNS OF SPIRITUAL DECADENCE

It was a beautiful spring morning. I was leaving on a trip the following day, so I wanted to make the most of the time with my kids. They were playing in our backyard and the sun was shining brightly. Everything was peaceful. I had awakened early and prayed for a while and was now enjoying the day with the boys. I had no way of knowing that mortal danger was lurking nearby.

After being together in the yard for a while, I told the kids, "Let's go for a bicycle ride." So we all climbed onto our bikes and went for a nice ride. We returned from the bicycle ride and the kids were again in the backyard, playing near a small children's swimming pool that we set up each spring when the weather gets warm. When the kids grew tired of playing, we all went into the house. Once inside, I noticed that the dog was barking insistently in the backyard.

I went to see what was wrong and could not believe my eyes. Right in the spot where my kids had been playing just moments before was a huge gaping hole over what had formerly been a dry septic well. The entire cement top which had been covering the well now lay at the bottom of the hole, eighteen feet down, covered by water.

Seeing the opening, I did not know if one of my children had fallen into the hole. I ran into the house in a panic and began counting heads, *One, two, three boys . . . Whew! Everyone is all right.* I gave thanks to the Lord for His protection over us.

By evening I was still shaken up by the thought that we had been so close to the danger, yet we had known nothing about it. Due to some heavy rains we had been having in Argentina, the earth in the well had washed away, leaving a hollow cavity underneath the concrete cover. To our natural eyes, everything looked fine. We could only see the green grass and the ground as it had always looked. But as the space was being washed out, it became a mortal trap which sooner or later was going to fall. My children were playing directly over it, and I did not have a clue.

Every so often we wake up to start another normal day and, without warning, something happens that alters the course of our lives forever. That is the way it is in the Christian life as well. Sometimes we do not realize that there are powers trying to eat away at the foundation underneath our feet.

This frightening experience caused me to meditate on lives that are not in tune with the Holy Spirit. It is critical that we pay attention to God's warnings in our lives. God gives us signs of danger to alert us to things that will wear us out, such as decadence or apathy. If we ignore the Holy Spirit, then in a predetermined moment a collapse will occur, and our lives will come crashing down.

SIGNS OF SPIRITUAL DECADENCE

Funk and Wagnall's Standard Dictionary defines "decadence" this way: "In the process of deterioration or decay; a condition or period of decline, as in morals." I want to share with you some warning signs of spiritual decadence that could help you avoid falling into a spiritual septic hole.

Lack of Spiritual and Moral Energy

A chronic lack of spiritual and moral energy can warn us of impending spiritual danger. I hear people say, "I am not a bad or destructive person. I do not harm anyone, but neither do I have strength to live a dynamic Christian life. I lack strength and motivation." Many people who lack motivation are living in a spiritual stupor.

Refusal to Change

Another sign of spiritual decadence is when we refuse to change. We bow down to the idols of stability and predictability. We do not want to be bothered by anything apart from what we already know.

Lack of Joy

I remember the first time someone confronted me about my lack of joy. A fellow student at Fuller Seminary approached me and said, "Sergio, are you a happy person?" I did not know how to answer her. I was going through a difficult time and was struggling with discouragement and loneliness. It was not easy for me to give her an honest answer. When there is no joy in the Christian life, it is a sign that something needs to change.

I am not saying there should never be any suffering or sadness or that you will never again have any problems. I am saying that even in the midst of pain and groaning, there can exist the joy of the Lord.

Becoming Too Controlling

Another sign of spiritual decadence is when we become control-ling. Typically, we want to be the owners of everything and do things our way, or we constantly defend our own rights. Another aspect of this problem might be an obsession with the accumu-lation of riches.

Living with Anxiety and Panic

Warning lights flash in the form of recurring moments of anxiety and panic. You may incessantly feel that something is wrong but do not know what it is. If you have this problem, God is speaking to you right now. He wants to prepare your heart so that He can pour His Spirit into your life.

Accepting Sin as Normal

Trouble sets in when a person thinks, *Well, it is obvious that I cannot overcome this vice. And since it has brought such a burden of guilt upon me, I will deal with it by choosing not to deal with it. When the temptation comes, I will give in to the sin and then forget about it.* Some Christians have signed a peace treaty with their sin. They have signed an agreement and said, "Look, since I cannot get rid of you, I will allow you into my house. But you need to stay low-key and not bother me too much."

Such misled individuals have no idea what sort of treaty they have signed. When these types of sins are allowed to take up permanent residence in our homes and lives, they bring nothing but destruction and disaster. The Holy Spirit is coming right now with a flashing red light and is saying to you, "Dear child, wake up! Wake up you who are sleeping and let Christ shine into your life!" If you have been ignoring these red warning lights, now is the time to receive the message God is trying to give you.

Boredom in Your Prayer Life

Some Christians are so disciplined that they pray even though they find it boring. Before they go to work, they take a half an hour for prayer. But they spend their time looking at the clock and making mental lists of things they need to do. Their minds and hearts are not even there.

Having Our Feet in the Church and Our Eyes on the World

A person may think, *I do everything I am supposed to do: I attend church, I pray* and so on. But their strongest heartbeat is not for the Church or the things of the Lord. The passions of their heart are somewhere else. They may think, *How wonderful it would be to be able to live like that.* Or they may exclaim, "What greatness there is out there!" The lights of this world have attracted them.

Withholding Our Finances from the Lord

Beloved brother or sister, are you withholding money that the Lord has placed in your hand to enrich and bless your local church and missions? If so, it could be a sign that you are in spiritual decadence. Maybe you do not love your church as you once loved it. Maybe something has grown cold in your heart and the Holy Spirit is flashing the red light, saying, "I do not see your generosity. Your offerings are no longer heroic like before."

Bothered by the Cross

When the words "sacrifice," "suffering" and "the cross" bother us, when we only want to hear messages about blessings and do not want to be told about suffering, our hearts are in need of a change. Many today will receive a message of prosperity and avoid calls to repentance and sacrifice. Some people do not want to hear about the blood of Jesus or His sacrifice because it sounds very stark and harsh. Even though they may know it was this very sacrifice that bought salvation and eternal life, they turn their ears away.

Addictions

Addictions are a strong sign of spiritual decadence. For example, social drinking is a common problem. Red lights flash when a person needs a drink to feel good or when he or she believes that relief for their soul is going to come from alcohol. The Holy Spirit is saying, "It is time that you do something about this!" It is time that you be free from your bondage.

Addictions come in all shapes and sizes. These include compulsive shopping, overeating, lurid romance novels, gambling, using illegal substances, selfish ambition and a lust for money. This list, of course, could go on and on. (I will touch on sexual addictions under "Hooked on Pornography.")

Fatalism

Another sign of spiritual decadence is fatalism. This is when people throw themselves into the hands of the future as someone would into a boat floating down a river without any destination. They think, *No matter what I do, I have a feeling that my life is going to end in failure. My grandfather was a failure, my uncles failed, some of my friends failed and I have a very strong feeling that I, too, am going to fail.* These kinds of thoughts are another sign that there is spiritual decadence and danger.

The Bible tells us that Christ has a plan for us and that the Lord has called us to go from victory to victory and from glory to glory. As children of God, our futures are bright and hopeful (see Jer. 29:11; 2 Cor. 3:18).

Hooked on Pornography

Pornography is a sin; it is corrosive and destructive. Some have said, "But this does not bother anyone else; it is secret and private. It is something that I do in my own mind or only in private moments." One day we will have to give an account before the Lord for every perverse act that we have done, seen or spoken. Pornographic magazines are printed in hell. Some people never purchase such magazines, but pornography's filthy fantasies pollute their minds just the same.

Unholy Entertainment

Another sign of spiritual decadence is when we indulge in entertainment that is not pleasing to God. Many believers live pure lives except when it comes to their private entertainment. It is as if they are saying, "Now I have special permission from the Holy Spirit to abandon purity and to leave behind my principles." It is during such times that they let themselves enjoy profane jokes or immoral videos that in other moments of their lives they would not accept. But since the joke or film comes with a dose of humor, they allow it into their lives and the lives of their families.

I want to take a moment to warn you that this type of thing erodes the earth and will cause the ground underneath your feet to one day to fall away and come crashing down. Such "harmless" entertainment *will* cause harm to you and your family.

Deadly Passivity

Passivity is when we have a very indifferent attitude about everything. One sure sign of spiritual passivity is emotional numbness, to the point where a person thinks, *Nothing interests me*. To those of you who struggle with this, I will tell you that something needs to happen in your emotions. You need to let the Holy Spirit touch the most intimate fiber of your heart. You may think, *I cannot even feel the presence of the Lord. I do not feel joy, nor do I feel sadness. I cannot laugh or cry.* God wants to heal your emotions. He wants to put His arms around you, renew you and touch you afresh.

GOD'S WARNING LIGHTS

The signs of spiritual decadence serve to warn us that something is wrong. They can be compared to the warning lights on the dashboard of a vehicle. The warning lights tell us if there is not enough oil, if the brakes are about to fail, if the battery is not recharging, etc. When the oil light comes on, for example, there are a couple of things you can do about that red light. One option is to take out an old rag from underneath the seat, cover the red light and forget about the problem until the motor freezes up and the engine is destroyed.

Our conscience and the voice of the Holy Spirit operate in the same way. Many times the Holy Spirit speaks to us and it is like a red light flashing a warning to us. He is giving us a signal that something dangerous is about to happen, and He points the way for us to set things straight before the disaster occurs.

So how can we fight against these things?

REVERSING THE CYCLE OF SPIRITUAL DECAY

The first step in reversing the cycle of spiritual decay is to renounce the vicious lie which tells us that a reasonably high percentage of holiness is enough. I have already shared my testimony of how the Lord grabbed me and shook me and sounded the alarms in my life.

All the red lights flashed before me and He said, "98% holiness is not enough."

I had thought everything was well with the Lord. I was living my life with a fairly high degree of holiness and I thought that was enough. God revealed to me, however, that when we do not walk in total obedience, even our occasional acts of obedience become offensive to Him. Isaiah 64:6 says, "All of us have become like one who is unclean, and all our righteous acts are like filthy rags."

Someone once said, "We do not give anything to God until we give everything to God." Many people have not given anything to the Lord because they have not given Him everything.

ASLEEP IN THE LIGHT

Years ago, the late Christian singer Keith Green sang, "The sinners are asleep in the darkness, while the Church is asleep in the light." What a strong statement this is and what a strong wake-up call the Holy Spirit is making today to all believers!

Probably the majority of the readers of this book are Christians who love the Lord. But the Lord is demanding more of His Church today. God is calling for a greater surrender of His servants because He wants to use us in new and powerful ways to advance His kingdom.

CHURCH GROWTH IS NOT A THREAT TO SATAN

It is time to leave behind the things that are a hindrance to our holiness and to open our hearts 100% to God. Some may say, "Yes, I know the Church is not perfect, but at least the Church is growing." I, too, say praise to God for that reality. When we see a country where the church growth rate is very high, we give glory to God. But I want to make a statement that is fairly radical: Church growth is not a threat to Satan. Church growth is only a threat to the devil when that growth is accompanied by holiness.

While the Church is pulling people out of the icy waters, the lifeboat itself is sinking.

The Church is like a lifeboat on a ship that is sinking in icy waters. When the Church lacks holiness, when the Christian family does not live in purity, when a believer has not looked for and tried to be like Jesus Christ, that lifeboat is full of holes. On one hand, the Church is pulling people out of the icy waters; on the other hand, the lifeboat itself is sinking.

I was in a country where the regional superintendent of a large Christian denomination did not quite know what to do with this message. But later, God touched his heart and he made this public confession:

> We have taken the gospel as a sport; it is like a hobby for us, and we are proud of the great growth that we have been experiencing in our churches. We have allowed ourselves to settle back and become lax and comfortable with our level of religiosity. We have experienced church growth without holiness.

Beloved brother and sister, it is good to continue to grow as a church, but it is best—and necessary—that we grow into the holiness of our Lord Jesus Christ.

Perhaps you recognized in yourself one or more of the signs of spiritual decadence that we just discussed. If one of those red lights is flashing on your spiritual dashboard, I beg you, in the name of Jesus, not to resist the voice of God. Kneel down in His presence and tell Him right now, "Lord, I want to consecrate my life to You and I know that I can live a life 100% in Your will."

HOLINESS IS TRANSFERRED, NOT WORKED UP

When I talk about 100% purity, I am not talking about human perfectionism or self-discipline. I am saying that the holiness of Christ can be imparted to us. First Corinthians 1:30 says: "You are in Christ Jesus, who has become for us wisdom from God—that is, our righteousness, holiness and redemption."

When you come to the cross of Christ, the purity and the holiness of God is imparted freely to your life. Lives that were once spotted and dirtied by sin now become purified. Lives that had been condemned by sin now are pardoned.

Some of you may be saying, "Pastor, I have heard this kind of message before. I am already familiar with it." I am not asking if you are familiar with it. I am asking you, in the name of our Lord Jesus, do you *practice* what you heard? Are you applying it to your life?

LET GOD SANCTIFY YOU!

Avoid every kind of evil. May God himself, the God of peace, sanctify you through and through. May your whole spirit, soul and body be kept blameless at the coming of our Lord Jesus Christ (1 Thess. 5:22,23).

Notice the sense of completeness in this passage. This scripture is for those who do not believe in the doctrine of complete holiness. It is a hammer of God that breaks the misconceptions of our hearts.

The key to avoiding spiritual decadence is this: Ask the Lord for *Him* to purify us completely and impart His holiness to us.

Not long ago I ministered to a young church-going man who was struggling with many different sins. He had allowed anger, profanity, rage, discord and pornography to enter into his life and now was struggling to be free. He repented and expressed his desire to change. Recently, I inquired to see how he was doing and he said, "I told the Lord, 'If You really want me to live a holy life, You will have to take the world out of my heart.' And you know what? God did it! I am completely changed and living in victory!"

The Lord desires that all of our being be holy—not only our soul and spirit, not only the religious aspects of our lives, not only on Sundays or days when we have church services. Temptations on this side of heaven cannot be avoided, but a passion for God can be so strong that it eclipses the blinding lights of temptation.

ABANDON ALL ELSE TO WALK IN PATHS OF HOLINESS

First He calls us, then He asks us to abandon everything else. He asks us to be broken and to give up our earthly desires. He says, "If anyone would come after me, he must deny himself and take up his cross and follow me" (Mark 8:34). This is a call to sacrifice everything in our lives on the altar of God. It is a call to say no to worldliness and follow Jesus Christ wholeheartedly.

But after such surrender comes His promise: "The one who calls you is faithful and he will do it" (1 Thess. 5:24).

I come to you with the conviction that Jesus Christ will do the work in our lives when we give Him permission to do it.

A few months ago a young man from my congregation asked me this question: "How long are you going to be preaching about holiness, Pastor?"

And I answered him, "Until the entire church has repented! Until the holiness of God is complete in the congregation." Why not believe that just as Jesus is the healer, He is also the sanctifier? Why not believe that all men, women and children can live in purity?

This type of commitment does not mean that we will never again commit any sin, because we are human and fragile. But we can say, "If I remain in the grace of the Lord, I can walk in paths of holiness." Because I sought holiness and I received sanctification by faith, I can affirm with Paul: "My conscience is clear" (1 Cor. 4:4).

How wonderful it is when we can stand firmly before the Lord and say, "My conscience is clear. By the grace of God, by the blood of Jesus Christ, I have been purified from all evil." The Lord puts His "treasure in jars of clay to show that this all-surpassing power is from God and not from us" (2 Cor. 4:7).

If you are a jar of clay, then you are a candidate to receive the impartation of the power of His holiness. Just ask for it and you shall receive it!

A CHANGE OF CLOTHES FOR THE HIGH PRIEST

The fire of holiness is a wonderful thing. But many people do not know what to do with this fresh move of God. They say to me, "How do I maintain this fire of holiness in my life?" Let us explore some key principles for receiving and maintaining the fire of God.

CAUTION: THE ACCUSER IS ALWAYS NEARBY

> Then he showed me Joshua the high priest standing before the angel of the Lord and Satan standing at his right side to accuse him (Zech. 3:1).

Observe this strange picture. Joshua, the high priest and principal pastor of Israel, is standing right in front of the angel of God. Then we see that Satan is standing at Joshua's right side. Even

Joshua, the mighty priest of Israel, is being accused by Satan.

Many believers live with the accusations of the enemy, just as Joshua did. Even as you read this book, you may be saying to yourself, *I feel a constant sense of guilt. I have repented of every known sin, yet I still feel guilty and I don't know what to do about it.* Remember, my brother and sister, a major ministry of the devil is to accuse Christians:

> Then I heard a loud voice in heaven say: "Now have come the salvation and the power and the kingdom of our God, and the authority of his Christ. For the accuser of our brothers, who accuses them before our God day and night, has been hurled down" (Rev. 12:10).

We are going to see what the Lord did about this. Some of you reading this book have the angel of the Lord standing right before you. But you also have the accuser at your right side. Many of you are still listening to the voice of the enemy. And even when you preach or teach, you do not experience complete freedom, because there are claims against you. These claims, however, are not from God. Satan is accusing the Church, marriages, ministries and individual believers.

Satan's goal is to make people feel dirty and to take away the good reputations of leaders. He will do all he can to undo the good moral conduct of some and to accentuate the filth of others. The Holy Spirit comes to convict of sin; Satan comes to flood us with unresolved guilt.

THE LORD REBUKES SATAN FOR US

Look what the Lord says in His Word: "The Lord said to Satan" (Zech. 3:2).

You can see here that the Lord did not speak first to Joshua. He spoke first to the devil. And the angel representing Jehovah Himself said:

The Lord rebuke you, Satan! The Lord, who has chosen Jerusalem, rebuke you! (Zech. 3:2).

The first thing we need to understand is that the Lord has chosen us. We are chosen people of God. We have a destiny, which means that the Lord has a glorious plan for our lives. In the kingdom of God there are no second-class citizens. Through the cross of Christ, we are all first-class citizens!

Because the Lord has chosen the Church, He rebukes the devil. Many committed Christians have a guilt complex that they think is the work of the Holy Spirit. But this kind of guilt never sanctifies, it only brings regret and sadness. It is a mental torture, but it does not purify us. This is the difference between condemnation (which is from the enemy and drives us away from God) and conviction (which is from the Holy Spirit and drives us into the arms of God).

The devil brings a very general sense of guilt. His goal is to make us feel dirty. But the Holy Spirit brings conviction of sin. The Holy Spirit is specific and wants to tear the sin out of our lives. He wants to remove whatever is left of the old life.

So the first thing the Lord does with Joshua is rebuke Satan, because the devil has no rightful place in Joshua's life. The Lord also does this for us.

Notice in this story of the high priest that the situation gets worse. The Lord says, "Is not this man a burning stick snatched from the fire?" (Zech. 3:2). You and I are burning sticks snatched from the fire of sin and captivity. The Lord has taken us out of captivity and has freed us from the filth of this world. But many

Christians are still smoldering and have a little smoke coming out of their lives. The Lord even wants to take that away.

Remember that Joshua and his fellow Jews were coming out of captivity in Babylon. As the high priest, Joshua was being accused of being incapable. Does this picture look familiar? Today many pastors and teachers disqualify themselves because they feel incapable and incompetent. When guilt-ridden people are given a ministry in the church, they risk using their position to get rid of their inferiority complex. They are burning sticks snatched from the fire.

A High Priest Dressed in Filthy Clothes?

"Joshua was dressed in filthy clothes as he stood before the angel" (Zech. 3:3). Similarly, our churches are filled with people dressed in filthy clothes. Many ministries are full of deceit, envy and the fear that they will lose their place of importance. Do you know what these are? Old garments. Some people travel from one Christian conference to the next, receiving from many different servants of the Lord and saying, "Lord, bless me as I am." But God cannot do that because their garments are vile.

The Lord wants to change our filthy garments and cause us to live with a completely clean conscience. It is possible. God can do it. And when the Church is sanctified, the gifts of God begin to manifest. Then the holiness of God begins to flow out into the streets and the power of God begins to touch the universities, schools, boardrooms and bedrooms.

No one needs to live a life of defeat, because God is saying to the devil, "I rebuke you. Let go of the Christians, let go of the Church." I pray that God would rebuke the accuser in your life. You are free! The Lord is doing a wonderful work in your life.

Those of you who have little faith, tell the Lord, "I believe. Help my unbelief and strengthen my faith." The fire of God is coming to all the nations. The spirit of holiness and power and the knowledge of the Lord will cover the earth as the waters cover the sea (see Isa. 11:9).

Thank the Lord for the revival that is coming over the world. Take a moment and pray this prayer:

Lord, do not pass me by. Use me. I do not want to be left standing on the sidelines. I want to be in the center of Your will. I am a burning stick snatched from the fire. Change my filthy garments today. Purify me, wash me and give me the authority that I need. Amen.

A Change of Clothes for the Ministry

The angel said to those who were standing before him, "Take off his filthy clothes" (Zech. 3:4).

So they removed the filthy garments from Joshua. God wants you to go through a crisis—a very precious crisis of holiness. He wants to put you, your family and your ministry through the fire of God so that He can transform what He wants to transform.

Zechariah 3:4 continues, "Then he said to Joshua, 'See, I have taken away your sin, and I will put rich garments on you.'" You may have already experienced the way God removes filthy garments; you might experience it as you read this book. But after your time of repentance, the Lord wants to give you rich garments.

Back to Joshua. Then "they put a clean turban on his head and clothed him, while the angel of the Lord stood by" (v. 5). A turban is like a cloth wrapped around the head. The turban in this passage represents the protection that God gives us over our thoughts. A significant number of Christians seemingly have control over many things in their lives but are unable to control their minds. When the fire of God comes over your life, it will bring authority and an instant reaction against sin.

HOLINESS IS NOT ONLY LOVING GOD, BUT ALSO HATING SIN!

And because I consider all your precepts right, I hate every wrong path (Ps. 119:128).

When the baptism of the Holy Spirit and fire comes over your life, it develops in you a very holy indignation against the power of sin. You will begin to hate every wrong and evil path. Holiness is not only loving God, but it is also hating sin. If you do not hate your sin, you will not be free from it. I pray that God would give you a perfect hatred for your sin.

> *The Lord is asking us to*
> *declare war on our sin.*

As we discussed earlier, some have grown accustomed to cohabiting in peace with their sin. But the Lord is asking us to declare war on our sin. Declare yourself an enemy of your alcoholism. Declare yourself an enemy of lust, pornography and domestic violence. Declare yourself a friend of God!

HOLINESS HELPS YOU FIND YOUR PLACE

How many saints are in the wrong place? How many of you can say, "Pastor, I am so frustrated. It seems like I do not fit in anywhere. People do not recognize me or value me. I do not even value myself." The Word of God tells us in Zechariah 3:7 that if you follow the paths of purity and holiness, the Lord will give you a place in the kingdom of God:

> This is what the Lord almighty says: "If you will walk in
> my ways and keep my requirements, then you will govern
> my house and have charge of my courts, and I will give
> you a place among these standing here."

SYMBOLIC MEN AND WOMEN CAN CAUSE CHANGE

> Listen, O high priest Joshua and your associates seated
> before you, who are men symbolic of things to come:
> I am going to bring my servant, the Branch (Zech. 3:8).

"Symbolic" in this verse refers to those who are a symbol or sign—an example or influence—of His righteousness. In the measure that Christian leaders and pastors walk toward the holiness of the Lord, their entire churches and congregations will be affected. Symbolic Christians today represent a genera- tion that has an all-consuming passion for God. When the

Church sanctifies itself, our cities will change and the world will tremble.

All Sin Removed in a Single Day

Says the Lord God Almighty, "And I will remove the sin of this land in a single day" (Zech. 3:9).

Very often, swift, dramatic corporate repentance happens during revivals. At the beginning of the 20th century, a revival of fire embraced the nation of Korea. When it began, the Lord removed the sin of the people involved in just a few short hours. On the first day of the revival, people spent the entire night standing in line waiting their turn to confess their sins. Beloved, we are hungry to see that day come in scores of cities around the world!

For that day to come, you and I need to renounce our filthy garments and let the angel of the Lord give us rich garments. And then the fire will descend and will take us all over the world with the gospel of Jesus Christ.

Some people say, "Pastor, I am not sure that I want to receive this fire. If it comes, I am afraid that I might lose it within a couple of days." Just as Claudio Freidzon told me when I first received this baptism of fire: "Beloved, this fire will never leave you."

Jesus, Remove My Filthy Garments Now!

I would like to invite every Christian who still has sin in their life to pause right now and pray. God is about to give you new and clean garments. This is not for just a few; the fire of God is for the entire Body of Christ. Come to Jesus and receive the baptism of fire now.

Take a few moments right now to remove any filthy thing that remains in your life. I declare to you that no vice, bad habit or bondage has more power than Jesus Christ. If you come to Jesus Christ, He will remove all your filthy garments. We are awaiting that day when you, through your church, invade your city and see thousands upon thousands kneeling at the feet of Jesus.

Some of you will receive a baptism of fire to win entire cities. Some of you will receive fire to win entire countries for Christ. You may be thinking, *I need Jesus to change my garments.* If God is convicting you, then do not hesitate. Take a moment right now and tell Him, "Jesus, remove my sin; tear away my filthy garments. Do whatever You wish in my life. Do what You want with me." I pray that the Lord would give you the blessed ability to groan for your sin. He is looking with pleasure at the offering that we are giving to Him: the offering of a broken heart.

Every person who needs to give up a relationship that is outside His will, take a moment right now and give it to Him. If there is still something that needs to be removed from your life, I invite you to read this prayer out loud, with sincerity of heart:

Thank You, Lord, for dying on the cross for me. Lord, I know that I can live a life of holiness and purity. That is why right now, I receive the holiness of Jesus Christ. Angel of the Lord, take away my vile garments and give me new garments. Give me garments of purity, holiness and joy. My Lord, forgive my sin and free me from my rebelliousness. Change my character, transform my conduct toward my family, my work and my church. Make me a new person.

Lord, empty me from everything that is mine. Cleanse my heart. Empty it out so that I may be prepared to receive the fire of holiness. Lord, I promise that I will take care of this fire; I will treasure it. I will keep it, with Your help, until the day of Jesus

Christ. I will hate sin and live a life of purity for You. I promise it, my God, in Jesus' name.

And now my Lord, embrace me with Your love. I receive Your mercy, grace, forgiveness, approval, purity and fire for my church and my city. I receive it now!

The Lord is accepting the offering right now. All work of the devil has been canceled, because the Church has sanctified itself. The Lord has rebuked Satan. There is no condemnation for those who are in Jesus Christ. Amen.

11

THE DYNAMICS OF TEMPTATION

have a burden for servants of the Lord. My desire is that their
fruit would remain and that they would be able to remain firm
in the Lord. The ministry of pastors, evangelists, prophets,
teachers and apostles is not to have a greater personal ministry
but, rather, to equip, perfect and prepare the saints for the work
of the ministry.

I want to share what the Lord, by His grace, has shown me so
that if you are in the ministry, your ministry would grow and
you would be affirmed. It is my prayer that one year from now
you will be doing better than you are today and that in five years,
if the Lord should tarry, you will be doing much better still,
always growing in the grace of the Lord. If you are not serving in
full-time ministry, please do not skip ahead to the next chapter.
The principles here apply to all believers desiring a greater ability
to resist temptation.

LESSONS ABOUT TEMPTATION FROM GENESIS 3

Genesis 3 speaks to us about temptation and how to defend ourselves against it. I want to share some of the dynamics of temptation and how to deal with them. Genesis 3:1-3 reads:

> Now the serpent was more crafty than any of the wild animals the Lord God had made. He said to the woman, "Did God really say, 'You must not eat from any tree in the garden'?"
>
> The woman said to the serpent, "We may eat fruit from the trees in the garden, but God did say, 'You must not eat fruit from the tree that is in the middle of the garden, and you must not touch it, or you will die.'"

HOW TO DEFEND OURSELVES AGAINST TEMPTATION

As long as we are here on earth, we will have to deal with the problem of temptation—always—even if we are in the midst of a great revival. Even if you are one of the best church workers in the world, you will have to deal with temptation. If you are not prepared to confront this problem, it is possible that the enemy will gain a victory in your life. How can we prepare? Let us look at some ways.

Know That the Enemy Is Insidious and Extremely Cunning

How does temptation work? First of all, temptation comes slyly because the devil acts with intelligence. The devil is not stupid. He comes with a diabolic and infernal shrewdness, and works to see if he can deceive us. If the devil is successful in capturing your attention and distracting you from God's direction, then he can gain control over your life. Satan cannot do anything to us, however, if we do not give him room! The problem is that by being human, we give him a place to work.

Know That Sin Is As Powerless As a Frozen Serpent

Sin is like a frozen serpent: It no longer has any strength or authority over us. The work was complete at Calvary. The problem starts when a Christian says, "Poor serpent, you must be cold," and puts the snake near the fire to warm up. That is when it revives. And when it revives, it attacks.

Do Not Converse with the Devil!

We see in Genesis 3 that the serpent was much smarter than all the other animals of the field. It came with shrewdness and spoke to the woman. Do you know what was the first problem? The woman decided to hold a conversation with the serpent! My father has a very powerful ministry of deliverance. Ever since my childhood, I can recall him teaching this principle: "Do not dialogue with the devil. Do not hold a conversation with the enemy."

Often as I minister, I sense in my spirit that some people in the audience cannot pay attention to my message because they are hearing other voices. At times I stop to ask for anyone hearing strange voices to raise their hands. It is amazing to see the number of people who respond.

Do you hear voices? It may even sound like the Holy Spirit to you, but in your mind, you know there is something in that voice that is not according to the patterns of the Bible. Do you have thoughts of suicide, even ideas that it might be a noble thing to do since you cannot fulfill your duties in life? Make sure that you reject that kind of advice. It comes straight from hell—reject it.

Ask the Holy Spirit to give you discernment. Check with mature Christians. Identify misleading voices. As Ed Silvoso says, "Do not let the demons teach you theology." We need to resist demons and cast them out. We can confidently even speak to Satan himself and biblically resist him, saying, "Satan, the Lord rebuke you" (see Zech. 3:2). We should not have an attitude of companionship with the enemy. We should be aggressive and develop a mind-set of war against him.

Discern Demonic Immorality

A pastor from Brazil shared this story with me:

> I had never struggled with pornography and lust in my life as a believer. It was just simply not one of my fights. Then a year ago, I suddenly began to be totally obsessed with lust and pornography. It was almost overwhelming. It felt like something coming from outside of me. Some pastor friends and I began to pray. Soon a convert from the occult came to me and told me that for the past year, ten Macumba (a satanic cult in Brazil) groups in this area had made a list of targets to destroy with immorality. He told me, "Your name is on all ten lists."
>
> Upon discovering the enemy's strategy, these people prayed directly against the darts of immorality. Instead of shrinking back with guilt and shame, I became assertive and turned my strength to resist satanic invasion. By God's grace, I succeeded.

Months later I visited this man's city for a conference. This pastor was baptized with fire in a spectacular way. I have had precious fellowship with him and I enjoy seeing him getting stronger as he ministers to others in the power of the Holy Spirit.

Some ministers feel guilty about their secret sin when, in some cases, the occult has been bombarding their minds. They need to distinguish between what is their own carnality and what is a direct attack and not be ignorant of Satan's schemes (see 2 Cor. 2:11). Confess your struggles to God, repent from any yielding to the lure of the enemy and resist Satan.

Be Aware of the Gradual Nature of Temptation

The problem is that the enemy comes very gradually and progressively. Just as the serpent crawls along the ground, so temptation slithers into our lives. It is similar to the laboratory experiment with the frog and the pot of water. A frog is placed into a pot of

Temptation is a gradual danger. You think you are fine even as the temperature is rising around you.

water. He can jump out if he wants. The pan is then placed on a burner, which is heated very slowly. As the temperature of the water rises, the frog still does not move. Gradually, the water turns to a boil and the frog dies. This experiment shows clearly the principle of gradual danger.

That is the way temptation works for many people. It is gradual and moves quietly and progressively. And once you allow temptation into your life, it will continue to eat away and gain a great foothold. That is why it is so important to put an end to thoughts and patterns that have slithered into your life. You must repent of them at the altar of the Lord. It is all too easy to think *I am fine* without even realizing that the temperature is rising all around you.

Many realize too late that they have given room to the enemy. Satan then traps them and causes great injury. Afterward there is forgiveness, grace and mercy, but how much more difficult it is for the one who fell! How much better it is to be able to say "Thank You, Lord, for keeping me and for protecting me." It is wonderful to be able to maintain a pure testimony and enjoy the protection of the Lord.

Unfortunately, Eve did not ignore the words of the devil and began to hold a conversation with him. The serpent came slithering by and asked her a seemingly reasonable question. He did not say, "Eve, do you want to sin today?" Rather, he said, "Did God really say, 'You must not eat from any tree in the garden'?" (Gen. 3:1).

> The woman said to the serpent, "We may eat fruit from the trees in the garden, but God did say, 'You must not eat fruit from the tree that is in the middle of the garden, and you must not touch it, or you will die.'"
>
> "You will not surely die," the serpent said to the woman (Gen. 3:2-4).

If the conversation had stopped right there, maybe Eve would have said, "You are a liar; I am getting out of here." But Satan did not bring only lies to her—rather, lies mixed with truth. He said:

> "You will not surely die . . . . For God knows that when you eat of it your eyes will be opened, and you will be like God, knowing good and evil" (Gen. 3:4,5).

In a sense, Adam and Eve were going to be like God because they were going to know both good and bad. They were going to lose their human innocence. What did Satan do? He brought them poison covered in chocolate, so to speak. He made his speech just intriguing enough so that Eve would say, "How interesting—what an appealing doctrine." And Eve began to doubt.

Learn to Wield Your Sword

How different it was for Jesus in the desert! Satan tempted Jesus with worldly desires: greatness, nourishment and fortune. In one minute, Jesus could have had all the kingdoms of this earth if he had knelt down before Satan (see Luke 4:1-13).

But the Lord said, "It is written," and He rebuked the devil with the Scriptures. On the other hand, Eve wavered and failed. Many insecure Christians sit in churches every week, participating in the service and perhaps even experiencing the blessings of God. Unfortunately, too often it only lasts as long as they are in the service. Later, they go to their homes, begin to waver and return to their previous spiritual states.

Do Not Waver in the Face of Temptation

One of the signs that a Christian is not well planted in the Lord is if they have a changeable character. The Bible says that he who is double-minded is unstable in all his ways (see Jas. 1:8). If he is a pastor, his strength will begin to diminish and he will dissolve his own ministry. He is like the waves of the sea: One day he is big, the next day he is not. He is insecure just as Eve was insecure.

Maybe Eve was like those believers who tell me, "I don't trust anyone. They lied to me and gave me a prophecy that did not come true. I have lost my faith in everything that is supernatural." Be careful, my brother and sister. May the Spirit of God protect you from raising barriers against the knowledge of Christ.

I am not bringing you a series of human or fleshly arguments but, rather, the admonition that the weapons of our warfare are not carnal but powerful in God for the destruction of strongholds (see 2 Cor. 10:4). The word "destruction" in the Greek also can mean to pulverize—to break down the strongholds that rise up.

These strongholds can take the form of wrong, or misguided, conclusions. They can be mental barriers that have risen against the knowledge of Christ and against the light of the Holy Spirit. Is it possible for a minister or church worker to have strongholds? Yes! When Paul was speaking about strongholds to the church at Corinth, he was talking to believers. In 2 Corinthians 10, when Paul talks about strongholds that have risen up against the Church, he is talking about invisible walls that are blocking part of the blessing of God.

Eve doubted and began to mix things. She wavered. Genesis 3:6 says:

> When the woman saw that the fruit of the tree was good for food and pleasing to the eye and also desirable for gaining wisdom, she took some and ate it. She also gave some to her husband, who was with her, and he ate it.

Do Not Become Awed by the World

Eve became intrigued by the words of the serpent. She was curious and wanted to taste that which was forbidden. Today, many people in the Church are struggling with the same issues. They are paralyzed by their sin. They think, *I am not going to do it*, but their heart is still there. They admire the world, they cherish it. Out of religious shame, some do not quite pursue the evil, but they say to themselves, *I wish I could*. They daydream of the things that are forbidden.

I was in Spain with some missionaries whom I love a great deal and who have been very influential in my life. We began to have a conversation about how nice the stores were in the United States, how much progress they had made as a nation and how we admired the things they had. I did not realize it at first, but we were being awestruck by the things of this world. The Bible does not say we cannot enjoy things in the world, because God put things like food in the world to be enjoyed. He gave us taste buds so we would be able to taste good foods. It is not wrong to enjoy such things, but it is wrong to love them.

While we were talking about this, my pastor friend began to recite 1 John 2:15: "Do not love the world *or anything in the world*" (emphasis mine).

I said to myself, *This is the Word of God for my life. It is a rebuke and challenge for my soul. I am going to change. I want to think differently.* I do not want to love what is in this earth, because it is all temporary.

Very soon, the eternal will come and that which is temporary will no longer matter. So we need to be careful that nothing steals our passion to the point of eclipsing our love for Christ. We must be careful that nothing would trap us or bind us.

Assume Responsibility for Your Actions

Part of the problem for Adam and Eve was that they did not assume responsibility for their actions. Why did Eve fall and invite her husband to join her? According to Genesis 3:12, Adam said to God, "The woman you put here with me—she gave me some fruit from the tree, and I ate it."

Men, we need to assume responsibility for the pastoral care of our homes and not shift responsibility to our wives. I often tell the men of our congregation, "Brother, the pastor of your home is *you*. The pastor of your wife and children is you." How important it is for us men to assume the spiritual responsibility of our homes!

Some of you may say, "Yes, but my wife is more spiritual than I am. I am more of a businessman, more administrative." In terms of spiritual leadership in the home, God is not concerned about

- what kind of temperament you have;
- what your manner of thinking is;
- whether you are left-brained or right-brained;
- whether you are a person who thinks concretely.

His direction is that you should assume the spiritual leadership of your home. If you assume this role, it will help you avoid many disasters and conflicts in your family.

The wife, Eve, also found a way to avoid responsibility for what happened:

Then the Lord God said to the woman, "What is this you have done?" The woman said, "The serpent deceived me, and I ate" (Gen. 3:13).

Sister, do not lay the blame on your destiny, your family members, your neighbors or the devil. The woman, too, has to assume her responsibility and understand that she is called to live a life of holiness. God is going to hold you responsible for your actions.

In conclusion, God wants us to be on the defense, protected and alert against the insinuations and attacks of the enemy and not ignorant of the schemes of Satan.

PREPARING THE ALTAR
FOR THE FIRE

We love to read in 1 Kings 18 about how the prophet Elijah confronted the priests of Baal and called down fire from heaven. My brother and sister, the fire does not fall in just any old place in the middle of the desert. We must prepare the altar of our lives if we want to be ready for the fire of God to fall upon us.

Before the fire fell for Elijah, he endured an arduous process of preparation. And what was God preparing him for? To change the religion of an entire nation in one day! Elijah's task was to pull the Jews away from the pagan worship of Baal and bring them back to their belief in one God, Jehovah the Lord. We read in 1 Kings 17:1:

> Now Elijah the Tishbite, from Tishbe in Gilead, said to
> Ahab [who was the king], "As the Lord, the God of Israel,

lives, whom I serve, there will be neither dew nor rain in the next few years except at my word."

Immediately a drought began in all of Israel. Then the Word of the Lord came to Elijah:

> Leave here, turn eastward and hide in the Kerith Ravine, east of the Jordan. You will drink from the brook, and I have ordered the ravens to feed you there (1 Kings 17:2-4).

God was saying, "I am preparing something. I am preparing the nation and with this drought, I am going to break them." Why did God choose a drought to break the obstinate will of His people? Why not an earthquake or some other method? Maybe it was because Baal was the god of rain, crops, prosperity and fruitfulness. With a drought, He was hitting Baal hard. God could say, "What kind of god do you worship if there is no rain? What kind of god of abundance and prosperity is this, if all your fields have dried up?" God was preparing the nation by sending a drought.

Be sure not to curse your drought, because sometimes dry seasons are from God. Many times He permits difficulties in our families, churches, cities and nations in order to prepare us and make us hungry for revival. When things do not work as they usually do, when there is discomfort, people often become more receptive to the Lord in their search for a solution.

STEPS IN THE PREPARATION PROCESS

We have to ask, How did God prepare Elijah to become the leader of a great revival in Israel? First of all, He told him to hide himself. He told him to drink from the brook of Kerith and to eat the food brought to him by ravens in the morning and evening.

Step 1: We Must Learn to Depend on God (Though His Methods May Be Strange)

God did not build Elijah a dining room. He did not give Elijah a telephone so that he could order out for pizza. The Lord said, "You are going to depend upon me and I am going to use methods that are unfamiliar to you. I am going to use one of those birds that are called 'unclean.'" Ravens were not considered clean by the Jews. The people of Israel kept their distance from these birds. Yet this was the very bird that God sent to take bread and meat to Elijah.

I can imagine Elijah sitting there next to the brook and wondering if the ravens were going to show up that day. There they came, morning and evening. He had direct food service sent by the Lord.

Step 2: We Must Be Willing to Change

> So he did what the Lord had told him. He went to the Kerith Ravine, east of the Jordan, and stayed there. The ravens brought him bread and meat in the morning and bread and meat in the evening, and he drank from the brook. Some time later the brook dried up because there had been no rain in the land (1 Kings 17:5-7).

How difficult it can be when God sends us to a place and says, "See this brook—you will drink fresh water here." We walk to the brook day after day and say to ourselves, *Yes, this is just as the Lord said it would be.* Then one day we go and there is less water. The next day, there is even less water. Suddenly we realize, *This brook is drying up!* Finally, one day it dries up completely; nothing is left of the brook.

How difficult these changes are for some Christians. They think, *But God sent me to do this ministry. God spoke to me 10 years ago! At first everything was fine, but now everything has dried up.* Brothers and sisters, this is a hard lesson for all of us. First, we have to learn to depend upon God. And second, we need to learn to change, as God leads us.

I teach this principle to pastors: The worst enemy of the revival that is about to come can be the previous revival. Those who were happy with the previous revival often want nothing to do with the new thing that is about to come. They are looking at Charles Wesley, John Wesley and Charles Finney and are expecting a dignified revival.

How many times do we hold on tightly to the previous blessings and say, "Lord, please do not move me from this place. I received this blessing exactly the way it is. It is my brook."

The Lord is trying to say to us, "I sent you to the brook, but now I am telling you to leave that place. I made it dry up so that you could no longer depend upon a mere stream. Now I am going to send a national downpour! With the brook, I could give you enough to drink, but the people of the nation are dying. I want to move you out of this hiding place so that you can defeat the Baals. As a result, I will send a downpour over the entire nation and bless it."

The Lord will do what it takes to move us out of our ministries and comfortable lives into a new place. We say, "But Lord, I was behaving well. I was working for You; You put me here." And many times we fail to see that it is *God* who wants to move us out of that old place.

He may reply, "Yes, I sent you there 10 years ago, but now it is time to move. I want to do something new with you." Brothers and sisters, let us not allow our previous obedience to become the enemy of our present obedience.

Elijah did not have much possibility of staying at the Kerith Brook, for if he had, he would have died. How many of you want the Lord to dry up the brook where you are camping? My prayer is, "Lord, dry up my brook so that I must continue to depend upon You." Even the brook can become a routine in our lives. I am sure that Elijah got used to drinking from the brook and waiting for the ravens to bring him his food, until the Lord said, "Enough. I am doing something new!"

God is not static. He is active among the human race. Because of His love, He is always working among us. So prepare yourself for change. We see the change that came in verses 7-9:

> Some time later the brook dried up because there had been no rain in the land. Then the word of the Lord came to him: "Go at once to Zarephath of Sidon and stay there. I have commanded a widow in that place to supply you with food."

Change places from where you are. Obey God's instructions.

Step 3: Go to the Places That God Tells You

We read in 1 Kings 17:9 that the Lord told Elijah to go to Zarephath of Sidon. Zarephath was to the north of Israel. But it was not even in Israel; it was in Phoenicia. The Lord said, "I am going to use you, but I am going to take you away from where you are. I am going to take you out of your comfort zone."

It makes me think about some of the members of our church who are accustomed to their cell groups. They are comfortable there; they go to receive and to find friendship. Strong bonds form. Then one day the cell leader says, "Brother, we are asking you to take the leadership course and to begin leading a cell. We have a group that needs you on the other side of town." Some would answer and say, "No, I am doing fine right where I am! I don't want to move. I am receiving here and being fed." But someone saw God's anointing at work in that brother and his capacity to be a leader.

Oh, but how comfortable it is to stay right where we are in our little corner, hidden next to our peaceful brook. But God is calling us to something greater. My brother and sister, God calls you to serve in His Kingdom.

The third step in the preparation process is to be in the right place. Sometimes it is tempting to question the place to which God is sending us. The Lord told Elijah to go to Phoenicia, outside of Israel.

Step 4: We Must Be Willing to Depend on Others

Some will not pass the test because they are unwilling to go where God wants them to go. What would have happened if Elijah had refused to leave Kerith? He could have said, "What do you mean a widow is going to feed me? God feeds me directly from the heavens. I am not going to depend upon a woman, especially a Phoenician who is not from Israel. She is a widow and she does not have any money. No!" How many Christians do the very same thing with the will of God for their lives?! Then they wonder why the fire does not fall and why the rain does not commence.

We have to be docile and sensitive to the will of God. Many times my wife and I have thought out loud, "What would happen if we just stayed in our local congregation, forgot the international travel and just worked with the leaders, workers and all the brothers and sisters here? I wonder if we could solve this problem or that problem." Sure, we could stay put, but we would be in disobedience. That is how the fire in *our* lives would go out. Then I think, *Lord, You have called me to the nations. I will continue going to the nations and pastoring until You say "enough."*

We need to be serious in our service to the Lord and in our commitment to Him. My heart is gladdened when I see the amazing commitment of some servants of the Lord. Time goes by and they continue serving year after year. They possess an ironclad stability and a consistent inner strength. They do not abandon their call, they do not hang up their gloves and they do not waver. They continue following the Lord. This is how Elijah was.

Step 5: We Must Be Willing to Humble Ourselves and Ask

We read about more about Elijah's journey in 1 Kings 17:10:

> So he went to Zarephath. When he came to the town gate, a widow was there gathering sticks. He called to her and asked, "Would you bring me a little water in a jar so I may have a drink?" As she was going to get it, he called, "And bring me, please, a piece of bread."

We see that Elijah stopped depending upon miracles directly from the hand of God. He humbled himself and said, "Dear Mrs. Widow, I am here on behalf of God. Would you please bring me some water and bread?" What a shame. The great servant of God who was getting ready to set all of Israel free from their idolatry was asking for a plate of food from a starving widow.

How many times does it happen that poverty does not affect us, but a fear of poverty almost destroys us? How many people have been broken, not because they did not have enough to eat, but because they did not understand the purpose of the Lord in their time of scarcity. They would have overcome and they would have survived, if they had continued following God. One way or another, He would have provided all they needed.

The terror and shame that comes through not understanding God's ways cause many to break down, to give up. They do not understand that sometimes we have to pass through tribulation, testings and struggles. They end up saying to themselves, *I am switching to another religion. I am going to find another place. I don't have enough food; I don't have enough water. I quit.* Walking with God is a faith enterprise. If we are going to continue and not lose our fire and our blessing, we have to walk by faith.

It was not that the woman did not have enough coins for her bus fare or credit to fill the gas tank of her mini-van. Her predicament was much more serious. She was in a nation that was beginning to die of hunger. The rain had stopped.

In the middle of this disaster, here was the servant of God asking for a little bit of water and food (of which there was not much). Sometimes God wants us to depend directly upon Him, and other times, upon special circumstances that He sets up. Perhaps you do not know where your next meal or tank of gas is coming from. You may be asking yourself, *What am I going to do with my finances? How am I going to make it to the end of the month on what I have?* Depend upon the Lord and upon what He can give you. Maybe He will give you another job. Maybe He will help you out in some other way. Maybe He will send someone your way to say, "Here, this is for you."

God is doing a new work. He wants to use us, but we have to be sensitive to His presence and do what He says. Elijah did not say, "Now that I am out of money I am going to go to such and such a church to ask for funds." No! The Lord told him, "Ask this widow; this is the woman who is going to give you what you need." When Elijah asked the widow for a little bread, she responded:

"As surely as the Lord your God lives," she replied, "I don't have any bread—only a handful of flour in a jar and a little oil in a jug. I am gathering a few sticks to take home and make a meal for myself and my son, that we may eat it— and die" (1 Kings 17:12).

What a situation she was in! She said, "Dear Mr. Prophet, I want to let you know that this is my last meal with my son, and then after this, we are going to die of hunger. All I have left is a handful of flour. I am making one last effort, using the last of my strength. Disaster is imminent." See how the prophet responded:

Elijah said to her, "Don't be afraid. Go home and do as you have said. But first make a small cake of bread for me from what you have and bring it to me, and then make something for yourself and your son. For this is what the Lord, the God of Israel, says: 'The jar of flour will not be used up and the jug of oil will not run dry until the day the Lord gives rain on the land'" (1 Kings 17:13,14).

If you are a pastor, I know how difficult it is to take up an offering when you know the people are in financial trouble. At times, perhaps, you have stood there and, based upon the sadness and pain, have wanted to say, "How can we advance in this work the Lord has given us? How can we even think of building to meet our needs?" How easy it is to give up and abandon faith when things look economically impossible.

Step 6: Fight Against Despair and Use Your Authority for Miracles
Verse 12 tells us that the woman had reached the end and was preparing to die. When you go out to do ministry and you begin

telling someone about the love of God, they may say, "Yes, but I have a terminal disease." It feels like your heart is falling down to your feet and you think, *How am I going to talk to this person?*

We need to draw strength in the midst of our weakness. We need to ask God to give us His strength, because the gospel is not temporal, but eternal. It can change the entire future of a person for eternity. Have the courage to pray for healing! We have many incredible testimonies of healings in our congregation. God is still healing today!

As you go out to do ministry, expect a miracle. When you knock on your neighbor's door to share with him or invite him to church, expect a miracle. Expect that people will be touched by the power of the Holy Spirit. If you are going to serve the Lord, you will have to fight against despair. Those who are not going to serve will not have to struggle with this. But those who *are* going to serve Jesus Christ will have to struggle against the desolation that exists in the world. Be careful that the desolation and the despair do not fill your heart.

If you let despair fill your heart, one day you will go to your small group and say, "We are all doing poorly. What is the point of continuing like this?" The believer, preacher, worshipper and intercessor will have to struggle against the demonic attack of despair, because the world is in despair. Are you willing to face it?

Notice that the widow says to Elijah, "Sorry, I cannot bring you food because I am just about to die. How can you ask me for food?" But also notice that Elijah does not say, "Oh, I am sorry. Forgive me for asking. I am going to knock on another door to see if they will give me some food." He told her, "Don't be afraid" (1 Kings 17:13). We need servants of the Lord who arise with authority and say to those in despair, "Do not fear."

Elijah had an opportunity to quench the miraculous and lean toward depression, disappointment and frustration. An attitude of dashed expectations could have immediately squelched his ability to perform miracles. But his docile spirit helped him cooperate with God's plan instead of creating resistance to it.

God is preparing you for great things.
Are you ready to expect miracles?

God is preparing you for great things. Are you willing to be docile and teachable? Are you willing to renounce your independence and link up with the Body of Christ as never before?

Step 7: Reject Self-Pity and Fatalism

> Some time later the son of the woman who owned the house became ill. He grew worse and worse, and finally stopped breathing (1 Kings 17:17).

The Lord had already done one miracle with this widow, providing food every day for Elijah and for the woman and her family. Elijah probably sighed in relief that the victory had already been won. Before he could celebrate, however, this long-suffering prophet had another crisis on his hands. After God's miraculous provision in time of famine, the son of the widow fell sick—a sickness so serious that he stopped breathing.

Some people endure a first trial, but when confronted with a "double whammy," they collapse. Their theology of perpetual prosperity and success leaves no room for seasons of consistent trials. Elijah was trained differently. His trials were painful, but they did not destroy his ministry.

Notice verse 18. It is also part of the preparation that God has for those who are going to do great things for Him:

> She said to Elijah, "What do you have against me, man of God? Did you come to remind me of my sin and kill my son?"

This is very difficult. How many cell-group leaders, pastors or even parents would have felt like running away in a situation like this? The woman was saying to Elijah that she believed the reason he came was to cause her misfortune. Be careful with your heart, your emotions and your affections. Before a great revival comes, the devil will come to see if he can destroy us emotionally.

During recurring crises, I have heard pastors conclude, "My church no longer needs me. In fact, these people would be better off without me and my preaching." If Elijah had not been prepared, perhaps he would have fled in this situation. He could have said, "Lord, I cannot serve You anymore. This is the last straw. You send me to poor people. You make an entire nation suffer hunger. And now I come to this home and it looks like I have brought them bad luck. The child has died!"

I ask you this sincere question: Are you ready to pay the price? Are you ready to remain firm even when everything around you falls apart? Do you have the kind of faith that can persevere?

> "Give me your son," Elijah replied. He took him from her arms, carried him to the upper room where he was staying, and laid him on his bed. Then he cried out to the Lord, "O Lord my God, have you brought tragedy

also upon this widow I am staying with, by causing her son to die?" Then he stretched himself out on the boy three times and cried to the Lord, "O Lord my God, let this boy's life return to him!"

The Lord heard Elijah's cry, and the boy's life returned to him, and he lived. Elijah picked up the child and carried him down from the room into the house. He gave him to his mother and said, "Look, your son is alive!"

Then the woman said to Elijah, "Now I know that you are a man of God and that the word of the Lord from your mouth is the truth" (1 Kings 17:19-24).

Notice that Elijah cried for his personal misery before the Lord, not before the woman. Why did God allow all these things to happen? I believe it was because He wanted Elijah's complete dependence upon Him. Can you see a crescendo in Elijah's faith and character?

At this point in the story, the prophet Elijah went before evil King Ahab. Elijah called a convocation of all the people and prepared the altar. Then the fire of God fell. Israel converted back to God and in one day, the religion of an entire nation was changed. God destroyed all the prophets of Baal, and then the rain began to fall.

Do You Want Revival?

How many of you want revival in your nation? God wants to use you. I do not know where you are in this process of preparation. Maybe you are resisting the changes. Maybe you are at a point where you want to depend solely on God and not on your brothers and sisters in Christ. Perhaps you do not ask for counsel or participate in any fellowship group. Maybe you are struggling with despair and disaster among your family members.

Whatever your struggles may be, Jesus is nearby and can give you strength. He is preparing you and those who stay in His army. Those who say, "Count on me, Lord," are the ones He is going to use in the end-time revival. Are you willing? Do you want to be used?

I pray that the same strength the Lord has given me would also flood your life. The normal state in life is to be unfaithful. But when the fire of the Holy Spirit falls upon the life of a servant, God gives him strength to take him forward. It is like an oil that never runs out; it just continues to multiply. Follow the leading of the Lord. If He tells you to change places, change. If He tells you to go, then go. How beautiful it is to follow the ways of the Lord. There is no comparison.

I pray that the Lord would seal this word in your heart. I pray that He would remove the anguish of death that some of you struggle with, even as you read this book. I pray that the Lord would remove that inner crying that says, "Lord, You are failing me." Believe me, brother and sister, the Lord does not fail you. He does not arrive late.

God is preparing you. He wants to put a resistance inside you that you have never known before. Maybe some of you have started and then quit dozens of things in your life. Right now, God wants to make you faithful, strong and firm until the very last day of your life. I pray that you would continue walking in this glorious way until the day the Lord Jesus comes to find us.

If you desire to prepare the altar to receive the fire of God, pray this prayer out loud and in faith:

Lord, remove from me the superficiality that destroys any lack of commitment to You. Father, affirm me in You like never before in my life. Lord, help me, so that when You ask me to go west of the Jordan, I will go to the west of the Jordan. When You ask me to change places, I will change places. Help me to go where You want me to go, O Lord. Father, I pray that You make me docile and obedient to Your Word and Your will forever. Amen.

KEEP THE
FIRE BURNING

An integral part of being Argentine is grilling and eating good meat. One of the most common social phenomena in Argentina is the *asado*—a meat cookout. The first cross-cultural encounters between Kathy and me happened on our honeymoon. We had chosen to spend our first week together in a cabin in Yosemite National Park. One afternoon, we decided to have a cookout for supper.

I began gathering the wood and just the right kind of kindling. I even chose some pine cones to use. Kathy sat nearby, observing me with wide eyes as I gathered a pile of things that I would need for our first cookout as husband and wife. I do not believe she had ever seen food cooked over a fire that was not built out of charcoal and lighter fluid.

You can imagine my intense desire to make that fire work, so we could cook our food and so my wife would be impressed by her industrious husband. After arranging it just right, I soon had a nice fire crackling. I find it a personal challenge to build the perfect fire, even today, for our cookouts.

FIRE, BURN BRIGHTLY!

Once the fire is started, I tend to say, "Well, that was the hard part; now I can relax." But sure enough, if I leave for a few minutes, the fire tends to die down. And that is the way it is with the holy fire of God. If we are not careful with this precious flame, it can become neglected. Following are some principles that will help you keep the fire of holiness burning in your life.

Believe the Lord Has Called You to Be Absolutely Pure

If you do not believe in the calling of purity, that is where the danger will come. Satan will persuade you that 1% or 2% sin is all right. He will say, "After all, you are on planet Earth; you are not expected to live a holy life." If you allow him, the devil will deceive you.

I pray that the Lord would give you conviction today and that your mind would be renewed. I pray that from this day until the day that Jesus comes, you will declare war against every kind of evil. You will need to become a terrible enemy of sin. You will need to fight it on all counts.

Some of you are afraid of this. You say, "I have heard people preach against immorality, and they ended up falling into immorality themselves." Sadly, in part this is true and you may think that those who talk too much about holiness will fall into sin. But you must know that many of those who fell were redeemed again and that many who preached against immorality their entire lives did not fall. Remember Moses? Elijah? Elisha? Daniel? Jeremiah? They preached fervently against sin and idolatry and, though they may have stumbled, they remained faithful.

The Word of God is our example; experience is not our rule. How can our experience give us the right answer if we have been on the wrong path with the wrong kind of understanding? That is like giving our car keys to an auto thief and asking him to keep an eye on our vehicle while we go shopping. Wrong experience—like an auto thief—cannot be trusted.

Do you believe the principles of the Word of God? Are you certain that Jesus truly came to earth, that His body was not made out of plastic, that He was real? Do you believe He endured temptation and hunger and yet did not say yes to sin on any account? If so, you are following the right path. When tempted by the enemy, Jesus said, "Satan, it is written." With the Word of the Lord, He fought sin and evil (see Luke 4). You can do the same thing. You and I are *called* to do the *same thing!*

Christian means "little Christ," follower of Christ, imitator of Jesus Christ. It has to be very clearly established in our hearts and minds: We are called to absolute purity, just like our model, Christ.

> May God himself, the God of peace, sanctify you through and through. May your whole spirit, soul and body be kept blameless at the coming of our Lord Jesus Christ (1 Thess. 5:23).

This verse is talking about complete and total sanctifying power. Our sanctification must be total, from our heads to our toes. Every cell of our bodies should be sanctified by the Word of God. Every thought and action should be purified by Jesus.

Some people say, "Pastor, I wish I could do this, but I am weak and shy and suffer from doubt." But:

The one who calls you is faithful and he will do it (1 Thess. 5:24).

The demands of God have not been lowered in this century. God demands that each one of us live in absolute purity. You can call it pride, you can call it excess, you can call it extravagance. But the Bible tells us: "May your whole spirit, soul and body be kept blameless" (1 Thess. 5:23). By the time Jesus comes, the whole Church should be pure, waiting in ready expectation for Him.

To keep humble, some people leave a little sin in their lives because they do not want to be too holy, too pure or too spiritual. Let me ask you a question: Can a human being be too pure before a holy God? Do you think God would say, "Don't come and pray like that; you are too clean. See if you can get some filth on you so you look more human, and then come back"?! God Almighty loves us and desires that we be totally pure.

How do we become holy? The One who calls us is faithful, and He will do it through us. It is in the power of the Holy Spirit that we become holy.

Keep Giving Away the Fire of God

If you receive a baptism of fire and all you do is stay home and do nothing about it, you will lose it very quickly. Why do they call the Dead Sea a dead sea? Because it takes in water from different rivers and streams, but it has no outlets. The water disperses only through evaporation, so the sea (technically it is a very large lake) accumulates salt. There is so much salt that no fish can live there. No tree can grow at its banks.

Some Christians are like the Dead Sea. They go to the best conferences and they receive and receive and the salt accumulates. But instead of being the "salt of the earth" (Matt. 5:13), they are the salt of themselves and they keep piling it up—more books, more tapes, more videos, more knowledge. They increase and grow but do not reach out.

Carlos Annacondia, the Argentine evangelist, says it so well: "If we want to keep the anointing, we have to keep giving it away." Every person in the Body of Christ is a minister. We are all called to be a special people of God, ministers and servants of the Lord God Almighty.

Understand That Holiness Is Not an End in Itself

My friend and mentor Ed Silvoso tells us why it does not make sense to pursue holiness as the ultimate end: "If the only thing God wanted from us was to be holy, then we might as well drop dead right now and be with God in heaven. We are going to be more holy there than we are anyplace else!" But the goal is not only to be holy, but to be holy *so that* we are a holy nation, a chosen people. We are a people special to God; we are set apart. For what? To *declare* the praises of Him who called us out of darkness (see 1 Pet. 2:9).

In the theology of holiness, we find two key aspects: separated from the world and separated to serve God. Separation must be accompanied by a dedication to serve.

Victorious Christian living is not only living on the defense, but it is also being armed and ready to advance. We cannot win a basketball game simply by staying close to the hoop to protect it. The best we could hope for using this tactic is a 0-0 tie. We have to run to the other end of the court and sink a few baskets to win the game.

The Baptism of Fire Is for the Fulfillment of the Great Commission

Every Christian has heard that the mandate of the Great Commission is to "Go into all the world and preach the good news to all creation" (Mark 16:15). Nothing will help us fulfill the Great Commission faster than receiving a baptism of fire. This baptism will restore your passion for God and lost souls. Those who get rid of their sin and receive the baptism of the Holy Spirit and fire will be in a place to allow Him to do His work in their lives.

A revival focused on the Great Commission will be a blessing as it brings the message of Jesus Christ to the world. The passage of Scripture that is known as the Greatest Commandment says (1) love God and (2) love your neighbor as yourself (see Matt. 22:36-40). The more we love people and the more we pray for them, the more the fire will burn in our own lives.

The fire that I received could have been lost within a few days. But the Lord opened opportunities and doors to share this fire and we took advantage of most of them. Whenever we had the chance, my wife Kathy and I walked through those doors and ministered to whomever we could.

Practice Personal Evangelism

How beautiful it is when you are sitting on a bus, train or airplane and God interrupts your agenda. You are getting ready to take a nap and you tell yourself, *I am so tired; I really deserve this rest.* But then the Holy Spirit tells you that you need to speak to the person next to you. You may say, *Lord, can I talk to them after my nap?* But you sense the love of Christ flowing through your heart. It is not just a command. You are looking for opportunities and if you are a little timid, you may pray, *Lord, have this person ask me what religion I am, or something like that.* Finally, something happens and the Lord provides the opportunity and you begin to talk.

As I shared earlier, in our ministry many people have received Christ on airplanes and in taxis. In Argentina, taxis are a way of life and typically, they are relatively inexpensive (at the time of writing this book!). Sometimes I say to myself, *I am not going to witness to this cabby because I need to rest on this short trip to the office.* And then the love of the Lord begins to flow. He loves people more than we ever will. Before I realize it, within two minutes I am in the middle of a big conversation about Jesus Christ.

I remember one young taxi driver who was taking me home. When we arrived at my house, he turned off the engine (rare for a cab driver!) and right there on my street asked me if I would pray with him. He received Jesus Christ sitting in his taxi!

Keep giving away to others the fire and blessings that you receive.

A few years back, the Lord impressed upon me that I had never witnessed to one particular neighbor. Finally I said, "I have got to witness to these people." So I knocked on the door and a lady answered. I said to her, "Do you know what the Lord has done for me? The power of the Lord came upon me and I was shaking under His mighty anointing." You and I know that unbelievers do not understand these things.

Nevertheless, she said, "Please come in. I need to hear this." She said to her daughters, "Turn off the TV. We need to hear this." For about an hour I witnessed to her and she came to Christ right there in her living room.

Even if you work in full-time ministry, do not let that deter you from the joy of bringing souls, one by one, to Jesus Christ. I know some leaders who tell me, "I do not have time to witness one-on-one. I will just spend my time speaking at large conferences." The Lord wants to break this type of professionalism and to remind us that we need to be led by the Spirit moment by moment. Keep giving away to others the fire and blessings that you have received.

Keep Your Passion Focused on God—Do Not Idolize Methods

At one time during those days in May 1997 when the Lord had me in His presence, He began to speak to my heart about making idols out of my methods. Then He sent me to speak to some pastors about church growth and how we must be careful not to abuse it. I was fearful to talk to these pastors about it, because I enjoy studying church growth. But the Lord showed me that some of those ministers were idolizing church growth to the point of it becoming their obsession and passion. (I use "idolize" here to mean "excessive admiration.")

On my knees, I cried out to the Lord and said, "Oh my God, many of us are looking toward Korea and the tremendous amount of church growth they have experienced. How can I go to these leaders and tell them to be careful about making an idol out of church growth?"

Do you know what the Lord spoke to my heart? He said, "My son, what I did in Korea cannot even be compared to what I am going to do on planet Earth in the coming years."

We have to believe in not only what God has done in the past but also what He is about to do in the future. God wants to bring a knowledge of His glory that covers the earth as the waters cover the seas.

Divine Intervention Outweighs Human Methods

Some of you may be thinking, *My church has doubled without ever experiencing a baptism of fire.* But can you imagine what would happen to your already-growing church if it were to receive this baptism of fire? Please, my friend, do not sell your spiritual birthright for a cup of lentil soup! Do not trade this fire for nice, steady growth. Pursue both, but know that a true baptism of fire generates true growth. Give priority to pursuing the presence of the Holy Spirit.

Normal church growth occurs when we share the gospel with the lost around us. It is wonderful and biblical. It is the law of God and we should continue doing it. But there is also a miraculous, explosive supernatural growth that happens when the Holy Spirit and fire descend upon a nation. It is not a method but a movement. The people in your neighborhood will begin to say, "Did you see what God is doing with those Christians?"

Do Not Give Up on Your Spiritual Dreams

How many of us have dreamt for years about a day when the move of God would be so great that you would have to stand back and marvel at His glorious work? It does not matter what kinds of barriers or failures you have experienced in the past. It does not matter if you are timid or afraid. It does not matter that you may have been a failure in the past. You must go to the source and receive this fire and authority.

If you go for the fire, you will need to be like Jacob when he took hold of the feet of the Angel of the Lord and said, "I will not let you go until you bless me" (Gen. 32:26). You must tell the Lord, "I am tired of working in my own strength. I want the strength of Your Spirit. I want to walk in the Spirit, be full of the Spirit and fire and have the mind of Jesus Christ. Lord, change my ministry!" He will do it!

Go to the Extremes for Holiness

Some of you might not struggle with sexual temptation. But

those of us that are very human have to be very careful. Often-times after a long, wonderful meeting, by the time I get back to my hotel room I am drained. I am physically exhausted and weak. I know that I am not a good fighter when I am very tired. Many of you can relate. We are human. On this side of heaven, we are vulnerable; our strength is limited.

Because of this human weakness, the Lord has helped me develop a habit that has been a blessing to me. No matter where I am in the world, the first thing I do when I enter my hotel room is drop my luggage, close the door, kneel down and ask God to take over that room. I pray for forgiveness for any fornication, adultery, immorality or pornography that has been present in that room before my arrival. Then I stand and command the demons that had legal right to stay in that room to get out. That room becomes the house of God while I am there.

I take one of those big towels or sometimes one of the blankets and cover the TV. And since I usually carry two Bibles, one in Spanish and one in English, I open one and place it on the TV, which then becomes the podium upon which I prepare my messages. The Bible says, "Flee from sexual immorality" (1 Cor. 6:18). This is one way of fleeing—refusing to watch TV while I am at a conference.

When I began putting a towel over the television in my hotel room, I felt good about it. I thought, *That is one less battle I will have to fight.* Some of you might be saying, "Why would you do that? What is wrong with TV?" I am not saying there is anything wrong with TV. There *is* something wrong with immorality, and there is a lot of immorality on TV. When I am exhausted, it is very hard for me to control the remote control. I do not trust myself that much. I trust the Lord and the Lord tells me to flee from youthful passions (see 2 Tim. 2:22). So I stay away from television when I am alone. Fight immorality with everything you have; the Lord will do the rest.

Make sure you clean your house of anything that is evil. The Lord tells us to go to extreme measures so that we do not fall into sin. Some of you may have a rough time controlling the cable stations on your TV. You may have the blessing of having many fine channels, but when you are alone, you cannot control what you watch. You say to yourself, *I am not going to watch this anymore.* Yet when you are alone, you end up watching it. Then you end up feeling so guilty, so filthy—I am talking about evil programs, not good programs.

I would like to share with you my paraphrase of Matthew 5:29: If the cable is giving you an occasion to fall, it is better to unplug the TV set and cancel the cable service and go to heaven without cable than to go to hell with a whole entertainment center around you!

Develop New Habits of Godliness

We need to change habits. Some experts say that it takes 16 days to change a habit. Some of you will have to work for at least 16 days, keeping a straight line until your flesh gets the message. You must commit that in His power, you are going to pursue righteousness, purity and holiness—and that you mean it! Until our minds are renewed, the old wineskins remain. But when we are renewed in our minds, the new wineskins come and the new wine is poured into the new wineskins. Job 31:1 says: "I made a covenant with my eyes not to look lustfully at a girl." We must do the same.

Preachers, teachers, evangelists, brothers and sisters (this is particularly for men, but it can also apply to women), today we must sign a covenant with our eyes. We have to tell our eyes, "You are never, ever going to look lustfully at a woman." If the person you are looking at is much younger, treat her as if she were your daughter and pray for her as a father. If she is not a Christian, pray for her salvation. If she is a woman your own age, treat her like your sister and with absolute purity. If you do not believe that you can keep such a commitment without help, then find an accountability partner to pray for you and support you.

As I have said before, no one would consider buying a bottle of water with a label that reads: "98% Mountain Spring Water, 2% Sewage Water." You would not decide, *Oh, this is great! It is almost pure. I think I will take it.* The Lord wants and demands 100% holiness from us.

Flee from Immorality

When you are running away from something or someone, you do not look very dignified. One time while waiting for a flight, a smiling young woman came walking toward me to talk to me. As she approached, I decided that I was going to witness to her. But something different was happening. As she was walking toward me, the Holy Spirit began to warn me, "I did not send this young lady to you."

The fear of God came upon me. Perhaps "terror" would be a more accurate word. I thought, *Lord, I do not want to become another casualty in Your kingdom.* So, as she came within a few feet, I turned around and literally fled in the opposite direction. She probably thought, *What is wrong with this guy?* I do not really care what she thought. I felt that I was fleeing from something that might have led to a compromising situation (see Gen. 19:17; Isa. 48:20; Jer. 51:6; 1 Cor. 6:18; 1 Tim. 6:11; 2 Tim. 2:22).

Run away from immorality, like Joseph did. Joseph the patriarch was determined that he was not going to commit adultery with Potiphar's wife. She then accused him falsely, and he lost his job (see Gen. 39). Some of you may even lose your jobs for walking straight with the Lord. You may lose some worldly riches when you refuse to lie or comply with evil. But do not worry. The Lord will repay you because He is faithful.

Did you know that you can be single and still be pure? The Lord will give you strength. When the Holy Spirit comes upon you, you will be very strong. You will know, *I am weak, but the Holy Spirit is strong in me.* Marriage does not cure the vice of lust; only the blood of Jesus does. But you need a heart with a disposition toward total purity.

Get Close to Anointed People

We have been so careful not to idolize other people that sometimes we do not make ourselves available to receive what they have to give us. If you know a brother or sister in your church who is ablaze with the fire of God, get close to that person. Make friends with the friends of the Bridegroom. The friends of the Bridegroom have lamps that are full of oil and are ready for the moment. Receive from these people and be renewed through them.

It is so powerful when God's children link together in unity and support. If you allow yourself to be vulnerable and to learn from Him and others, the Lord will bless your life and your anointing will increase. You will not lose it. When you think you are losing it, one of your friends will come, guided by the Holy Spirit, and say, "How are you doing? Let's pray together."

If you desire to walk in His purity, take a moment and pray this prayer right now:

God, forgive me for departing from the teaching of holiness. Change my thinking. Help me to believe that Jesus died for my sanctification. Lord, I declare that I can be pure, because Jesus has provided sanctification to me. Lord, I receive the gift of purity, in every area of my life.

The Lord is putting a mark in your heart. With the power of the Holy Spirit, He is sealing the concept that you and I will walk in absolute purity the rest of our lives. Some people say, "Pastor, what happens if I pray today and then tomorrow I fall into sin again?" You kneel down wherever you are and say, "God, forgive me and purify me." If you have to do it 100 times a day, do it 100 times a day. The Lord will purge you of your sin. He will give you victory and a ministry full of His power.

Some of you may have serious doubts about whether you were destined by God to have this fire. You may think, *Well, I wasn't born in Argentina* (i.e., a place of ongoing revival), *so maybe I will not receive the fire.* The Lord will always say yes to those who want the Holy Spirit and fire. What I have, I want to give to you. Even as I write these words, I pray that the baptism of fire which I have received would come upon each and every one of you that asks for it and truly desires it.

Together with that fire comes a responsibility to serve God in your city. Are you ready? Are you willing? Please pray this prayer:

Lord, I promise I will use this fire of holiness to minister to the needy, the poor and the sick; to those who don't know You; to my relatives, my friends, even my enemies. Jesus, I promise to use this fire for the glory of Your name and for the extension of Your kingdom. Amen, amen and amen.

We have been taken out of mediocrity and called to be heroes for Christ. Some people desire that the Lord would do something great and that He would do it beginning with them. The Holy Spirit told me that He wants us to die to the pride of originality. Some people try to come up with a strategy that is "original" to them and for that reason they will not cooperate with the strategies of others. Some wonder why they do not triumph.

Just take hold of Jesus Christ and you will triumph. But you cannot do it with pride. Be holy!

HOW DESPERATE ARE YOU FOR THE FIRE?

ome time ago, I was invited to preach at a conference which was to be held in another country. Actually, I was not the original preacher invited to the conference. Shortly before the event, the original speaker informed the organizers that he would be unable to make it. So they called and asked me to fill in for him. I agreed, as the Lord had confirmed in my heart that I should go.

Because my flight was delayed, I landed just in time to get to the service. As I entered the building, I was told that it was almost time for me to speak.

The leaders, however, took a long time making announcements and doing business before introducing me as the speaker. As I stood up to bring my message, the director of the conference leaned over to hand me the microphone and said, "Brother, you have only nine minutes left to preach." I took a deep breath and decided that I would preach my message as fast as I could. At least the people could hear a little bit of my testimony.

I also realized that the welcome was not too hearty. Perhaps the people were a little disappointed because the first preacher had been unable to attend. They did not know me or my ministry, except through the recommendation of some missionaries. But even though the atmosphere was a little cool, the Lord had a surprise prepared for all of us that night.

INTERRUPTED BY THE HOLY SPIRIT

As I took the microphone, I began speaking very fast. But as I spoke, there was someone who was talking louder than me. The Holy Spirit was speaking to my heart, even as I was trying to get into the sermon. Very clearly He said, "Stop preaching now." I struggled with what I was hearing. It was as if I was arguing with the Holy Spirit, even while I was trying to preach. Finally, the moment came when I could not even concentrate on what I was trying to say.

I said, "Brothers and sisters, please forgive me, but I cannot preach anymore. The Lord wants to do something else here." The most difficult part was that I did not even know *what* it was the Lord wanted to do!

I asked the people to bow their heads in prayer. Then the Lord said to me, "Call everyone forward who is thinking about death, struggling with suicidal thoughts or hearing voices even as you preach." I obeyed immediately. In less than three minutes, some 60 people had come forward. Something in the spirit world had been destroyed miraculously, even as the people came forward. In one moment the Lord had performed a mass deliverance, and the glory of the Lord fell in that place.

Many times we want to do things according to what we already know, but God wants to interrupt. That night I learned that often the Lord is saying, "Preacher, step aside. Today I want to speak directly to the people." The Lord wants to speak to us about breaking our religiosity—not our religion, but our religiosity.

RELIGIOSITY: AN UNCLEAN SPIRIT

Religiosity is an unclean spirit; it is a spirit of mockery toward the things of God. It is a spirit that comes to many churches to make fun of the genuine move of God. It is a spirit that binds people with empty routines.

On the second day of this conference, several church authorities and important leaders were seated on the platform. I was very careful and respectful in my preaching that day, and as I made the altar call, I read Psalm 51.

As we read that psalm together, the glory of God descended so strongly that it became impossible for me to stand up. I took hold of the pulpit to support myself, but its base was not strong and the entire podium fell on me as I fell to the ground. You can imagine how embarrassed I was. I tried to get up, but I could not.

I thought, *Lord, why is this happening to me?* I could see the feet of the superintendent and other dignitaries next to my head. And the Lord spoke to me and said, "My son, stay where you are. I am using you to break the spirit of religiosity that was in this conference." People in the conference began asking forgiveness of one another. Some of the leaders on the platform went down and hugged people in the audience, humbly asking their forgiveness. Repentance took place between the missionaries and national pastors for wrongdoing and bitterness. The atmosphere of the entire conference changed completely as the glory of the Lord came down. That night, the spirit of religiosity was broken in that place and unity and joy began to flow.

The Faith of the Canaanite Woman

Matthew 15 records the story of the Canaanite woman. She truly seems to have been in the wrong place at the wrong time, yet she received a powerful miracle from the Lord. She ended up being recorded as a woman of great faith. Jeremiah 29:13 typifies the faith of the Canaanite woman: "You will seek me and find me when you seek me with all your heart." The full story of the woman from Canaan is told in Matthew 15:21-28:

> Leaving that place, Jesus withdrew to the region of Tyre and Sidon. A Canaanite woman from that vicinity came to him, crying out, "Lord, Son of David, have mercy on me! My daughter is suffering terribly from demon-possession."
>
> Jesus did not answer a word. So his disciples came to him and urged him, "Send her away, for she keeps crying out after us."
>
> He answered, "I was sent only to the lost sheep of Israel."
>
> The woman came and knelt before him. "Lord, help me!" she said.
>
> He replied, "It is not right to take the children's bread and toss it to their dogs."
>
> "Yes, Lord," she said, "but even the dogs eat the crumbs that fall from their masters' table."
>
> Then Jesus answered, "Woman, you have great faith! Your request is granted." And her daughter was healed from that very hour.

As we look at this passage in Matthew, we see that the disciples had become very religious, even as they stood right next to Jesus. They already had their rules and their agendas. Jesus and the disciples had ventured northwest of Judea, to the pagan region known as Tyre. Jesus wanted a time of rest and privacy. The parallel text in the book of Mark tells us that Jesus had gone to a house to hide Himself and to be alone with His disciples (see Mark 7:24). It was not a day in which He was out ministering to the masses that regularly gathered to hear Him.

TRYING TO GET IN WITHOUT CREDENTIALS

But in this moment of rest, a Canaanite woman found Jesus and asked for His help. She came with many disadvantages. First, she was a woman. In Israel in those days, women were expected to keep quiet and to remain a little distant. Second, she was a Canaanite of Greek descent. She was not a part of the sheep of Israel; she lacked the necessary credentials. She was not part of the 12, nor part of the 70, nor part of the 500; she had no part with the people of God.

The Israelites looked down upon others who were not of their bloodline or race. They called all other peoples and nations Gentiles, and sometimes they even called them dogs! They spoke of them as pagans who did not know God.

Also, she was in the wrong place at the wrong time. Jesus was not preaching or conducting a crusade. Jesus was withdrawing. Needless to say, this woman found herself at a disadvantage as she gathered up the courage to approach Jesus for a blessing. But come she did, crying out, "Lord, Son of David, have mercy on me! My daughter is suffering terribly from demon-posses-sion" (v. 22).

TRAUMA DEMANDS AN ANSWER

Do you know why she cried out? This woman had a terrible problem at home. Her daughter was suffering horribly from demon possession. It was torture because she felt the pain of her daughter, but she could do nothing about it. Then she found out that Jesus was in that vicinity. When there is trauma in life, the Lord uses it so that we cry out—"Lord, Son of David, have mercy on me"—and seek His presence. Some people grow very bitter and sad when they go through trials. But God allows some of our trials to cause us to glorify the name of Jesus.

Some think, *I wish I would have been born somewhere else or in a different family.* Others believe, *If I had not had so much abuse in my childhood, then I would be a happy person.* They have regrets in their hearts for who they are, where they grew up and where they belong. But look what this woman did during the time of her storm. She came to Jesus and began to break the rules of religiosity. She did not say, "The Lord is Jewish, and I am a pagan woman; He won't have anything to do with me." She came to Him because her daughter was suffering.

Even if your family is doing well, your neighborhood and your city are suffering terribly from demonic attack. Entire nations are under the ruling authority of Satan; the Lord wants to change them once and for all.

THE SILENCE OF GOD

Upon hearing about this woman's problems, verse 23 tells us that Jesus did not say anything. How difficult it is when we hear only the silence of God. It is like picking up the phone, dialing a number, hearing a loved one say, "Hello?" and then hearing only silence. Sometimes the Lord delays His answer and His first answer is silence.

When there is pride in the heart, we get offended if heaven does not turn its ear toward us. We feel that God should answer us immediately. Maybe some of you have been experiencing the silence of God. These moments of silence are to test the hearts of His children and to see if there is enough faith in you to receive a miracle. At the silence of Jesus, many others have drawn away from Him. But this woman came to the Lord and though she heard nothing, she was determined to receive something from God.

RELIGIOSITY AMONG THE DISCIPLES

To make matters worse, the disciples said, "Send her away, for she keeps crying out after us" (Matt. 15:23). When we are overtaken by a spirit of religion, how easy it is to forget about human suffering! Here we find the disciples of Jesus saying, "Lord, this woman is causing us inconvenience. Tell her to leave." The answer that Jesus gives to the woman is even stronger and colder.

I can just picture this desperate woman, standing just a short distance from Jesus, looking at Him expectantly for a positive response. She is waiting patiently to see if the disciples are going to allow her to approach Jesus. He responds to His disciples and says, "I was sent only to the lost sheep of Israel" (Matt. 15:24). In other words, He was saying, "I am not in Israel at this moment; I am not with my people. And besides, she is not one of them. I cannot attend to her right now."

I know the Canaanite woman must have seen what was happening and heard the comments. She knew she was not welcome. She felt despised and rejected. Maybe it was time for her to turn her back on Jesus and seek answers from another religion.

But there was something in this woman that helped her to keep persisting. What would you have done in her place?

I Cannot Attend to You Right Now

Many people say, "Lord, I have faith in You," but their faith only lasts for 15 minutes. There are those who have stopped believing in many blessings of God—divine healing, the baptism of the Holy Spirit, the possibility of Jesus raising people from the dead, the possibility that believers can pray for the sick and see them leave their hospital beds. Their faith begins to diminish because one day they heard the Lord say to them, "I was sent only to the lost sheep of Israel." Do you know what Jesus was doing to the Canaanite woman? He was testing her heart.

We Need Faith and Perseverance

Do you realize that it is not enough just to have faith? This woman already knew very well that Jesus had the power to heal her daughter. She had faith. But what we also see in her is perseverance. The kingdom of God is for those who are violent, and the violent take it by force (see Matt. 11:12). You need a certain audacity of faith to receive a miracle from God.

This story of perseverance is repeated throughout the Bible. In Luke 8:43-48 we learn about the woman who had the issue of blood. She hemorrhaged for 12 years and had spent all her money seeking a remedy. She was physically, emotionally and financially ruined. She probably said to herself, *If I can just touch the border of His garment, I know I will be made whole.* With much difficulty, she pushed and shoved her way through the crowd until she reached Jesus and touched His garment. In that instant, she was healed. Her perseverance, mixed with faith, made her healing a reality.

DON'T GET OFFENDED BY GOD

When the Canaanite woman said, "Lord, help me!" look at the response of Jesus: "It is not right to take the children's bread and toss it to their dogs" (Matt. 15:26). What would you have done in this situation? Some probably would have gone home offended that night. I run into many people who feel offended by God. They say, "God does not love me. I seek God, and He gives to others, but I don't receive anything." Could it be that God is testing your faith and perseverance?

Jesus' response was very strong: "It is not fair to take the miracles that I have for the people of Israel and give them to foreigners like you." Brother and sister, do not back away when you are seeking God for a miracle. When you talk about your nation being "taken" for God, it will be taken by people who say, "This land will be a blessed land. Every corner of this land will feel the presence of God!"

If you are looking for an abundant harvest, you are looking for a good thing! But first of all, you need to immerse yourself in the presence of God. Like the Canaanite woman, you must come to the Master and say, "Master, I am not giving up. I came to receive a miracle from you, and here I am. I am seeking, searching and asking." Sometimes the answer from God will be very strong for us. The Canaanite woman had faith and perseverance, but the Lord still answered her very sharply.

Some of you have experienced painful religious traumas. Maybe your pastor or someone in spiritual authority has failed you and you have become resentful. Since then your spiritual life has not been full of the fire of God. You began closing yourself off, quenching the fire, unable to forgive.

HUMILITY, THE WINNING INGREDIENT

The Canaanite woman could have thrown herself a great pity party that day. She could have returned to her house and said, "I am going to stay home offended. Look what the teacher from Nazareth said to me. I am going to look for another religion." But hear what she said to the Master:

> "Yes, Lord," she said, "but even the dogs eat the crumbs that fall from their masters' table" (Matt. 15:27).

In those times, it was not uncommon for dogs to eat what had fallen from the table. Their masters did not allow them to eat directly from the table, but they could eat what fell to the floor. This woman was saying, "Lord, even if it is just the crumbs, please give them to me. I will take even a crumb of a miracle if it will help relieve the suffering of my daughter." We should say, "Lord, if I cannot sit in the front row, I will still take whatever You give me, even if it is from the back row. If they do not let me enter from the main entrance, I will wait on the sidewalk or in the parking lot. I want to receive what You have for me."

This woman not only had faith and perseverance, but she also had humility. She persisted and the Lord answered her: "Woman, you have great faith! Your request is granted" (Matt. 15:28). We all want to hear God say these words to us. But before He will, there has to be brokenness and a renunciation of pride and self-reliance. We must be ready to surrender our own schedules, agendas and personal aspirations. When we come to Christ, we kneel before Him and say, "Lord, I know You can do it, no matter how much resistance I face. I know You are the God of miracles."

If you want to receive His holy fire, you must be willing to be transformed.

To receive His blessings and holy fire, you must be willing to undergo a transformation. God is in the business of transforming the transformed. So if you have been transformed, do not think that this message is not for you. God wants you to be transformed again. He is changing those who have been changed. If your life has been going through a series of changes, I want you to know that the Holy Spirit is not finished with you. He wants to change us and keep changing us until we grow into the measure of the stature of the fullness of Christ (see Eph. 4:13). Our goal is Christlikeness. If you are not there yet, you and I should be growing to become more like Him everyday.

Do you want a formula that allows you to receive from God? Here is the biblical formula: faith, perseverance and humility. Do you want to see a miracle of God in your church? Do you want to see hundreds of souls converted to Jesus Christ? Do you want to see a powerful move of God in your city? No matter which evangelistic program you may choose to use, the first and most important ingredient is to seek God with faith, perseverance and humility.

THREE DYNAMIC DIMENSIONS

The Church has the power to invade planet Earth with the gospel. But something is hindering the Church worldwide from impacting nations with greater force than we are seeing in the present. It is *not* lack of resources. The early Church had much less than we have. Nor is it lack of technology. It could be the partial holiness syndrome, which is identical to the partial sinfulness syndrome in the Church.

We need a new outpouring of the Holy Spirit in the Church today. Nothing will advance the cause of the Great Commission more than the fire of God in its purity, power and passion for souls.

I suggest to you three dimensions in which we can live our lives in the Holy Spirit:

First, become a *seeker of the fire*. Make it a lifelong journey to seek God.

Second, become a *fire carrier*. As you continue to seek Him, allow the Holy Spirit to descend upon you mightily. You cannot produce this, but you can live in constant readiness for it to happen. It is impossible for God to deny you His Holy Spirit if you genuinely wait on Him. Once you receive the fire of His holiness, carry it to others. Do all the good you can. Relearn to do ministry in the power of God.

Finally, become *fire-carried*. Get to a point where you are so surrendered to God that He finds no resistance. The fire of God will guide you. You sense you are led by the Spirit and carried by His power. This maturity will not come automatically. It is not an event but, rather, a relationship and a lifelong process. To dwell in this level of glory is certainly awesome. On the other hand, this is not spiritual extravagance; it is wholesome Christian living and an intimate friendship with God.

As you live this kind of lifestyle, you die not only to evil but also to good things. When you give God everything, remember that whatever you enjoy in life is a gift from Him—your future, your career and your ministry must remain constantly upon the altar of consecration.

APPENDIX

SCRIPTURES THAT HELP US LIVE IN PURITY

Gen. 17:1 When Abram was ninety-nine years old, the LORD appeared to him and said, "I am God Almighty; walk before me and be blameless."

Lev. 10:10 You must distinguish between the holy and the common, between the unclean and the clean.

Lev. 11:45 I am the LORD who brought you up out of Egypt to be your God; therefore be holy, because I am holy.

Lev. 20:26 You are to be holy to me because I, the LORD, am holy, and I have set you apart from the nations to be my own.

Deut. 18:13 You must be blameless before the LORD your God.

Deut. 23:14 For the LORD your God moves about in your camp to protect you and to deliver your enemies to you. Your camp must be holy, so that he will not see among you anything indecent and turn away from you.

2 Sam. 22:26,27 To the faithful you show yourself faithful, to the blameless you show yourself blameless, to the pure you show yourself pure, but to the crooked you show yourself shrewd.

Ps. 15:1-3 LORD, who may dwell in your sanctuary? Who may live on your holy hill? He whose walk is blameless and who does what is righteous, who speaks the truth from his heart and has no slander on his tongue, who does his neighbor no wrong and casts no slur on his fellowman.

Ps. 84:11 For the LORD God is a sun and shield; the LORD bestows favor and honor; no good thing does he withhold from those whose walk is blameless.

Ps. 101:2 I will be careful to lead a blameless life—when will you come to me? I will walk in my house with blameless heart.

Ps. 119:1-4 Blessed are they whose ways are blameless, who walk according to the law of the LORD. Blessed are they who keep his statutes and seek him with all their heart. They do nothing wrong; they walk in his ways. You have laid down precepts that are to be fully obeyed.

Ps. 119:9 How can a young man keep his way pure? By living according to your word.

Isa. 35:8 And a highway will be there; it will be called the Way of Holiness. The unclean will not journey on it; it will be for those who walk in that Way; wicked fools will not go about on it.

Ezek. 44:23 They are to teach my people the difference between the holy and the common and show them how to distinguish between the unclean and the clean.

Dan. 11:35 Some of the wise will stumble, so that they may be refined, purified and made spotless until the time of the end, for it will still come at the appointed time.

Dan. 12:10 Many will be purified, made spotless and refined.

Matt. 5:48 Be perfect, therefore, as your heavenly Father is perfect.

Matt. 19:21,22 Jesus answered, "If you want to be perfect, go, sell your possessions and give to the poor, and you will have treasure in heaven. Then come, follow me." When the young man heard this, he went away sad, because he had great wealth.

Rom. 6:19 Just as you used to offer the parts of your body in slavery to impurity and to ever-increasing wickedness, so now offer them in slavery to righteousness leading to holiness.

Rom. 12:2 Do not conform any longer to the pattern of this world, but be transformed by the renewing of your mind. Then you will be able to test and approve what God's will is—his good, pleasing and perfect will.

1 Cor. 1:8 He will keep you strong to the end, so that you will be blameless on the day of our Lord Jesus Christ.

1 Cor. 1:30 It is because of him that you are in Christ Jesus, who has become for us wisdom from God—that is, our righteousness, holiness and redemption.

2 Cor. 5:15 Those who live should no longer live for themselves but for him who died for them and was raised again.

2 Cor. 13:11 Finally, brothers, good-bye. Aim for perfection, listen to my appeal, be of one mind, live in peace. And the God of love and peace will be with you.

Eph. 1:4 For he chose us in him before the creation of the world to be holy and blameless in his sight.

Eph. 5:1 Be imitators of God, therefore, as dearly loved children.

Eph. 5:26,27 To make her holy, cleansing her by the washing with water through the word, and to present her to himself as a radiant church, without stain or wrinkle or any other blemish, but holy and blameless.

Phil. 1:9,10 And this is my prayer: that your love may abound more and more in knowledge and depth of insight, so that you may be able to discern what is best and may be pure and blameless until the day of Christ.

Phil. 2:15 So that you may become blameless and pure, children of God without fault in a crooked and depraved generation, in which you shine like stars in the universe.

Phil. 3:12 Not that I have already obtained all this, or have already been made perfect, but I press on to take hold of that for which Christ Jesus took hold of me.

Col. 1:22 But now he has reconciled you by Christ's physical body through death to present you holy in his sight, without blemish and free from accusation.

Col. 1:28 We proclaim him, admonishing and teaching everyone with all wisdom, so that we may present everyone perfect in Christ.

1 Thess. 4:4,5 That each of you should learn to control his own body in a way that is holy and honorable, not in passionate lust like the heathen, who do not know God.

1 Thess. 4:7 For God did not call us to be impure, but to live a holy life.

1 Thess. 5:22,23 Avoid every kind of evil. May God himself, the God of peace, sanctify you through and through. May your whole spirit, soul and body be kept blameless at the coming of our Lord Jesus Christ.

1 Tim. 2:8 I want men everywhere to lift up holy hands in prayer, without anger or disputing.

1 Tim. 4:12 Don't let anyone look down on you because you are young, but set an example for the believers . . . in faith and in purity.

1 Tim. 5:22 Keep yourself pure.

2 Tim. 2:20-22 In a large house there are articles not only of gold and silver, but also of wood and clay; some are for noble purposes and some for ignoble. If a man cleanses himself from the latter, he will be an instrument for noble purposes, made holy, useful to the Master and prepared to do any good work. Flee the evil desires of youth, and pursue righteousness, faith, love and peace, along with those who call on the Lord out of a pure heart.

Titus 1:6,7 An elder must be blameless. . . . Since an overseer is entrusted with God's work, he must be blameless.

Titus 2:12 It teaches us to say "No" to ungodliness and worldly passions, and to live self-controlled, upright and godly lives in this present age.

Heb. 10:22 Let us draw near to God with a sincere heart in full assurance of faith, having our hearts sprinkled to cleanse us from a guilty conscience and having our bodies washed with pure water.

Heb. 12:10 Our fathers disciplined us for a little while as they thought best; but God disciplines us for our good, that we may share in his holiness.

Heb. 12:14 Make every effort to live in peace with all men and to be holy; without holiness no one will see the Lord.

Heb. 13:18 We are sure that we have a clear conscience and desire to live honorably in every way.

Jas. 1:27 Religion that God our Father accepts as pure and fault-less is this: to look after orphans and widows in their distress and to keep oneself from being polluted by the world.

1 Pet. 1:15 But just as he who called you is holy, so be holy in all you do.

1 Pet. 1:16 Be holy, because I am holy.

1 Pet. 2:9 But you are a chosen people, a royal priesthood, a holy nation, a people belonging to God, that you may declare the praises of him who called you out of darkness into his wonderful light.

1 Pet. 2:12 Live such good lives among the pagans that, though they accuse you of doing wrong, they may see your good deeds and glorify God on the day he visits us.

2 Pet. 1:4 Escape the corruption in the world caused by evil desires.

2 Pet. 2:20 If they have escaped the corruption of the world by knowing our Lord and Savior Jesus Christ and are again entangled in it and overcome, they are worse off at the end than they were at the beginning.

2 Pet. 3:11 Since everything will be destroyed in this way, what kind of people ought you to be? You ought to live holy and godly lives.

2 Pet. 3:14 So then, dear friends, since you are looking forward to this, make every effort to be found spotless, blameless and at peace with him.

1 John 2:6 Whoever claims to live in him must walk as Jesus did.

1 John 2:15 Do not love the world or anything in the world.

1 John 3:3 Everyone who has this hope in him purifies himself, just as he is pure.

1 John 3:6 No one who lives in him keeps on sinning. No one who continues to sin has either seen him or known him.

1 John 3:9 No one who is born of God will continue to sin.

1 John 4:17 In this world we are like [Jesus].

Rev. 22:11 And let him who is holy continue to be holy.

Rev. 22:14,15 Blessed are those who wash their robes, that they may have the right to the tree of life and may go through the gates into the city. Outside are the dogs, those who practice magic arts, the sexually immoral, the murderers, the idolaters and everyone who loves and practices falsehood.

SCRIPTURES ON THE NEED FOR CONFESSION AND REPENTANCE OF SINS

Ps. 119:128 Because I consider all your precepts right, I hate every wrong path.

2 Cor. 7:1 Since we have these promises, dear friends, let us purify ourselves from everything that contaminates body and spirit, perfecting holiness out of reverence for God.

2 Pet. 3:14 So then, dear friends, since you are looking forward to this, make every effort to be found spotless, blameless and at peace with him.

1 John 1:9 If we confess our sins, he is faithful and just and will forgive us our sins and purify us from all unrighteousness.

Scriptures that Tell Us Purity Comes Not Through Our Own Efforts

Lev. 20:8 Keep my decrees and follow them. I am the LORD, who makes you holy.

2 Sam. 22:33 It is God who arms me with strength and makes my way perfect.

Ezek. 11:18-20 They will return to it and remove all its vile images and detestable idols. I will give them an undivided heart and put a new spirit in them; I will remove from them their heart of stone and give them a heart of flesh. Then they will follow my decrees and be careful to keep my laws. They will be my people, and I will be their God.

Zech. 3:9 I will remove the sin of this land in a single day.

1 Thess. 3:13 May he strengthen your hearts so that you will be blameless and holy in the presence of our God and Father when our Lord Jesus comes with all his holy ones.

1 Thess. 5:23,24 May God himself, the God of peace, sanctify you through and through. May your whole spirit, soul and body be kept blameless at the coming or our Lord Jesus Christ. The one who calls you is faithful and he will do it.

Heb. 10:10 And by that will, we have been made holy through the sacrifice of the body of Jesus Christ once for all.